C000083806

THE POWER TO WIN

ACHIEVING PEAK PERFORMANCE WITH HYPNOSIS AND NLP

Laura Boynton King

THE LYONS PRESS
Guilford, Connecticut
An imprint of The Globe Pequot Press

To buy books in quantity for corporate use or incentives, call **(800) 962–0973, ext. 4551,** or e-mail **premiums@GlobePequot.com.**

Copyright © 2004 by Laura Boynton King

ALL RIGHTS RESERVED. No part of this book may be reproduced or transmitted in any form by any means, electronic or mechanical, including photocopying and recording, or by any information storage and retrieval system, except as may be expressly permitted in writing from the publisher. Requests for permission should be addressed to The Lyons Press, Attn: Rights and Permissions Department, P.O. Box 480, Guilford, CT 06437.

The Lyons Press is an imprint of The Globe Pequot Press.

Credits:
Photographer: Allan Carlisle Photography
Illustrator: Lila Blakeslee
Models: Tiffany Cornacchio, Brianna Martinez, Renee Hutchings, Heather White, Kathy Mulford, and Laura King
Designer: Stephanie Doyle

10 9 8 7 6 5 4 3 2 1
Printed in the United States of America

ISBN 1-59228-395-0

Library of Congress Cataloging-in-Publication Data is available on file.

For my mother, Helen Jean Boynton, for supporting me and believing in me every step of the way.

For Dorothy Gates, Ph.D., who has been my guardian angel for most of my life. Through her teachings and guidance, I am who I am today.

CONTENTS

Acknowledgments   vii

Introduction   ix

Part I: The Tools   1

Chapter 1: Hypnosis: What It Is, How It Works,
and Why You Need It   3

Chapter 2: Neuro-Linguistic Programming:
What It Is, How It Works, and Why You Need It   31

Chapter 3: The Laws of the Universe
and the Natural Laws of the Mind   49

Part II: The 6 Keys to Winning for the Equestrian   65

Chapter 4: Basic Relaxation
Your Physical State: From Tension to Relaxation   67

Chapter 5: Positive Self-Talk
Your Self-Talk: From Negative to Empowering   89

Chapter 6: Gaining Concentration
Your Focus: From Scattered to Optimal Concentration   109

Chapter 7: Release of Performance Anxiety
Your Emotional State: From Anxiety to the Zone   123

Chapter 8: Fearless Showing and Jumping
Your Mental State: From Fearful to Fearless   139

Chapter 9: Peak Performance
Your Expectations: From Mistakes to Peak Performance   153

Part III: Putting It All Together   171

Chapter 10: Developing Your Own Scripts   173

Chapter 11: Goal Setting and Achieving   191

ACKNOWLEDGMENTS

I especially want to thank my husband, Ed, who has supported me working as many hours as I have needed and is always willing to handle the responsibilities of our lives. I appreciate and love him for always being there for me. Thanks to our exceptional children, Larissa and Edward, for all the encouraging thoughts and phone calls sending me love.

I'd like to thank my mom, Helen Boynton, who has been the backbone of everything I have done. I have boundless gratitude and love for her. I thank my grandmother, Ruth Wedgworth, for allowing our family to be blessed with the magnificent gift of Lake Summit—Heaven on Earth—a place of inspiration and peace. God bless you.

I want to thank my sister, Kathy, and brother, Wayne, for always listening. Being the youngest of the family has been an amazing place to be because they are always there to take care of me.

I am a product of every method in this book. I first learned many years ago about hypnosis and I continue to learn and I thank my teachers. A special place is in my heart and mind for my mentor, Dorothy Gates, Ph.D., for being there many years ago and sharing her vast knowledge with me. I am sending a special thank you also to: Gerald F. Kein, Bob Brenner, Dr. Wil Horton, Calvin D. Banyan, Wendi Friesen, Kevin Hogan, Joan King, and Ron Eslinger. I have learned so much and I'm so grateful.

I've wanted to help people my whole life and I've always known that this book was part of the path God has put me on. I'm a sum total of all the experiences and know that I'm *on purpose* now. Over the past few years my friends have all been there for me no matter what I've been working on. My special group, SOS: Regina, Lili, Sheryl, and Nancy, I thank you all. During our special meeting the possibilities of what I could accomplish became real and obtainable. Many thanks also to Janet, who actually made the proofreading process fun.

Thanks Heather and Sheryl, who were there with their time, knowledge, and experiences, and helped me get it all together. You mean the world to me. Please always stay a part of my life.

There has been one person who is full of information and a source of knowledge. Her encouragement and positive attitude was there the whole way through. I have a huge attitude of gratitude for Mary . . . Special love and thanks for always sharing with me her insights and thoughts.

It is so fitting that my first book is about horses. Horses have been a passion for my whole life. I have loved the feeling that I have received by just having them as part of my life. Thank you, Dad, for giving me the love of horses. I miss you.

Last but not least . . . to a very special person who listened to all the scripts and critiqued them all every time I wrote or recorded one: Kathy, I am grateful for our friendship. Thanks for always hanging in there with me. We have shared our love for horses in our lives and we always will.

I am grateful for this opportunity to share *The Power to Win.*

INTRODUCTION

Hello, my name is Laura King, and in addition to being a horse nut, I am also a Certified Hypnotist, a Certified Sports Hypnotist, and the founder of Summit Dynamics Center in Wellington, Florida. I also have my Master's Practitioner certification in Neuro-Linguistic Psychology. When I began studying hypnosis almost 25 years ago, I had no idea that my passion for helping people and my love of horses and equestrian sports would one day come together. Today, my company is the world's only supplier of a comprehensive self-hypnosis program designed to help equestrians of all levels and riding disciplines reach their goals.

Hypnosis is a proven, time-tested way to help you achieve all of your goals. Millions of people have benefited from its power to help them make positive changes in their lives, including notables such as Tiger Woods, Albert Einstein, Jacqueline Kennedy Onassis, Henry Ford, Muhammad Ali, Kevin Costner, and Wolfgang Amadeus Mozart.

Hypnosis can help you transform bad habits, such as smoking, eating unhealthy foods, or biting your fingernails into good ones such as saying thank you, exercising, taking better care of yourself, and being more aware of what you need to do for yourself. It can help you turn your negative or sad feelings into positive, happy ones. It can help you effortlessly focus on almost anything in your life that you would like to change, while leaving you unburdened by analytical or pessimistic thoughts.

And, of course, it can help you improve your riding performance, from the inside out. Just as your coaches and trainers help you improve your riding skills and techniques by guiding you through physical rehearsal, you can improve your confidence and focus by guiding yourself through mental rehearsal. Hypnosis will help you get more out of your lessons because you'll be better able to do what your trainer asks you to do. You can get rid of your past fears, concentrate better, and believe in yourself so you can have peak performance. You will eliminate any mental or subconscious barriers to complete mastery of your sport.

You'll find that hypnosis does more than help you have a better seat, a better ability to cope with your challenges (either in the dressage ring or the jump ring), and smoother lead changes or the right distances to your fences. It helps you understand yourself better. In fact, it helps you become your real self. When you start to relax, the things you do to prevent you from being your real self go away and what's left is your real self. The chatter stops. You become more comfortable with your riding and with yourself.

Because what's inside you and what's outside of you are equally important in achieving optimal performance, if you are seeing a trainer, don't stop. Neither this book nor my 6 Keys to Winning for the Equestrian CD series is a replacement for your trainer's technical know-how. Instead, it's complementary—it helps you apply your lessons much more quickly, thoroughly, and confidently. It allows the brain to actually do what it is being taught, effortlessly.

My guess is that if you're reading this book, you're a person who wants a life full of peak experiences, and especially peak performance. This book will start you (or further your progress) on a journey to the place inside your mind that can create any experience—any future—you desire, one thought at a time.

I organized this book the same way I organize my seminars: by first explaining the tools I use—Hypnosis, Neuro-Linguistic Programming (NLP), and the Natural Laws of the Mind—and then by showing you how to combine them to produce peak performance in your riding, no matter what your level or discipline. I've included real-life stories to illustrate how hypnosis and self-hypnosis have helped my clients improve their riding and achieve higher levels of performance than they previously thought were possible (and that thought process was usually a big part of the problem, but we'll get into that later).

The *6 Keys to Winning for the Equestrian* program is a series that allows riders to experience the benefits of hypnosis in the privacy and comfort of their homes. The underlying principle behind the series is that the more relaxed and confident you are as a rider, the more you will enjoy what you're doing. And the more you enjoy riding, the more successful you will be. Each of the chapters in this book is based on one of the CDs in my *6 Keys to Winning for the Equestrian* program, and each targets a critical area of your subconscious mind to create quick, easy, effortless positive change. You will learn how to hypnotize yourself to achieve the same results you'd achieve if you were listening to the CDs or if I were sitting across from you.

The subconscious mind is most receptive to positive messages when in a state of deep, comfortable relaxation. In this state you can take your riding to the next level by making yourself confident, fearless, and focused—by making suggestions to your subconscious. In your first self-hypnosis session, Basic Relaxation, you'll learn breathing techniques that cultivate deep physical and mental relaxation. Muscle tension is replaced by peace and harmony, producing smooth, effortless, and relaxed body movements for a more pleasurable ride or competitive event.

Positive Self-Talk will help you conquer your enemy within. We're all our own worst enemies; we are capable of creating and/or perpetuating a lifetime of negativity all by ourselves, beginning with that gray stuff between our ears. Replacing negative self-talk with empowering, confident, uplifting language is a crucial step in the retraining of your brain.

The third self-hypnosis session in the series puts you on the path to success by helping you to improve your powers of concentration. Your ability to concentrate is bolstered by exercises that help you increase your self-awareness and self-discipline. Gaining Concentration gives you the ability to compete, despite the presence of potential distractions around you or in your mind.

There are very few athletes in any sport who have never experienced some form of performance anxiety. In equestrian sports, these fears are often amplified because all eyes are on you and your horse. Release of Performance Anxiety, the fourth session in the *6 Keys to Winning* series, uses mental imagery to help you replace feelings of anxiety with feelings of being a winner. Anxiety arises from thoughts about the outcome of the class you're riding in, of a future that you cannot control. When you release performance anxiety you're able to gain satisfaction from the process of preparing and competing, a process that, unlike the outcome, *is* within your control.

The fifth session in the series, Fearless Showing and Jumping, addresses the fear, self-doubt, and even terror some riders experience as a result of some real or imagined challenge. It helps you acknowledge and release those fears, and includes Blowing Your Fears Away, an exercise my clients find useful and even fun.

The final self-hypnosis session is called, simply, Peak Performance, and it is based on two key concepts. First, visualization is essential to success. All great athletes rehearse their performances in their minds to create the results they desire. Through the repetition of hypnotic suggestion, you can communicate with your subconscious mind and program your equestrian experience for success. Second, peak performance is achieved only after you are able to build confidence, poise, and self-image.

The most important concept I wish my readers to understand is the reason for the success of my clients is not me: it's them. Hypnosis is really something you allow to happen; you technically do it to yourself. All hypnosis is really self-hypnosis. You have within you—right now—the power to change almost anything you want about your thoughts and behavior.

How to Use This Book

Part I gives you an overview of the essential tools for the Power to Win; they are at the core of the effectiveness of what I do with my clients. Chapters 1 and 2 introduce you to hypnosis and NLP, but are by no means thorough explanations of either. If that's something you desire, any bookstore and, of course, the Internet will have oodles of information on both subjects—they are both well researched and well documented. My purpose is to briefly explain why they work so well. Chapter 3 explains what have been called the "Natural Laws of the Mind" and the "Laws of the Universe." They come from various philosophical traditions and disciplines, and they are not exhaustive. They are the kernels of wisdom that guide me in my practice.

Part II explains the *6 Keys* in detail, including many examples from my own experience as an equestrian and from my clients' experiences. I'm sure you'll find yourself somewhere in the stories, as I have yet to see a new problem or mistake.

Part III contains annotated scripts that illustrate how the principles of hypnosis and NLP and the Natural Laws of the Mind can all be incorporated to make optimal use of your time and deliver optimal impact to your subconscious. You'll find them particularly helpful when you are ready to create your own self-hypnosis scripts for whatever else you would like to change in your life. Finally, Chapter 11 provides a step-by-step process for setting and achieving your riding goals using self-hypnosis. At the end of Part III, you will have a customized plan to achieve the outcomes you desire for your riding, including timelines, action steps, and affirmations.

About the Graphics in *The Power to Win*

In order to reinforce the words on the page, I've included illustrations, photos, and icons to help you remember what you are reading. When it comes to memory, we humans need all of the cues we can get to help us retain information. Words + pictures + illustrations + icons is a powerful combination to get the most out of a single reading of *The Power to Win*.

Enjoy your journey, and remember that peak performance is just a thought away.

—Laura King
Wellington, Florida
April 2004

PART I

The Tools

CHAPTER 1

HYPNOSIS:

What It Is, How It Works, and Why You Need It

Before I get into the specifics of improving your performance, I'd like to explain hypnosis: its history, what it is, how it works, and why you need it. Hypnosis can help you understand yourself better; it can help you change your bad habits into good ones and it can transform your negative feelings into positive ones. And it can make these changes occur so easily that it sometimes seems more like magic than a scientific tool. If you want to know how and why, read on . . .

The slightly sinister-looking man asks you to have a seat. He takes out his pocket watch and holds it up, inches from your eyes, and tells you to look at it.

Its rhythmic, pendulum-like movement quickly mesmerizes you: back . . . and forth . . . back . . . and forth. "You are getting sleepy," *he says.* "You are getting sleeeeeeepy." *Soon you have been lulled into a trance, and you are under his spell.* "When I count to ten," *he says,* "You will lose all memory of who you are and you will assume the identity of . . . your mother-in-law."

That might work on the big screen, but the reality of hypnosis when it is used for therapeutic purposes (as opposed to a stage show) is that you are always in control. If you are seeking hypnotherapy as a way to improve your performance—and your life—your hypnosis session will no doubt be a lot less dramatic than anything Hollywood has ever concocted. Contrary to popular belief, the hypnotist has no magical power and cannot control you or make you do things you don't want to do. Hypnosis is a completely voluntary act wherein you always remain conscious; you're always aware and able to hear, to talk, and to make decisions.

So you can't turn me into my mother-in-law?
No. But I can help you transform yourself into someone who is more in-tuitive, more effective, and more successful.

How do I know it'll work for me?
Anyone of normal intelligence can be hypnotized, and you can only be hypnotized if you want to be and you willingly follow the hypnotist's in-structions. There are definitely people who are more or less hypnotizable than others, and also more or less willing than others. But most people fall right in the middle once they understand what it's about and realize that it's safe and it's going to help them. They comfortably go into a state of re-laxation and hypnosis and are receptive to the suggestions of the hypnotist.

Think of your hypnotist as a guide. If you choose to follow your hypno-tist's instructions, you will be guided into a wonderful, relaxed state of focus and awareness. And afterwards, you will remember everything that happened.

Do you really wave a pocket watch in front of my face?
Actually, many hypnotherapists use a pocket watch. And some even use a crystal, which few people are able to turn away from because the facets are so mesmerizing. The only prop I use for induction in my practice, though, is my voice. All you really need is a willing subject and a therapist with a calm-ing voice who knows how to take the subject into a deep state of relaxation.

How do I know I've really been hypnotized?
Actually, at the time you probably won't think you were hypnotized at all. Most people realize that they were indeed hypnotized after they've seen the desired changes in their behavior.

What will I feel like when I'm being hypnotized?
I can't say for sure, as everyone is different. Some people tell me they don't feel any different. Others tell me that they feel very relaxed and heavy, like a lead weight. And then there are the lucky ones who feel like they are floating on a cloud and they feel better than ever before.

How is hypnosis different from meditation?
The goal of hypnosis is to change behavior through direct suggestion. Al-though there are myriad types of meditation, the goal is usually the

quieting of the mind, a concentration on a specific state (e.g., compassion, forgiveness, love, death), or relaxation of the entire being. Although a change in your mental (or even physical) state is involved, the goal, per se, is not to alter your behavior.

How is hypnosis different from therapy?
Assuming there is no hypnosis involved, therapy appeals only to the conscious mind. It enlists the help of the intellect to solve problems and relieve stress. When you appeal to the conscious mind you can undoubtedly gain a lot of knowledge. But the more reasoning and intellectualizing you engage in, the greater the tendency to rationalize, to develop alibis, and to *protect the subconscious from changing your behavior.*

What if I get stuck in hypnosis and can't get out?
You can never get stuck in hypnosis because you have the power to emerge yourself at any time. All you have to do is tell yourself that you are emerging.

Why do I need hypnosis?
When you're in a hypnotic state you can easily make positive changes because your subconscious mind is more open to suggestions for change. To really understand why and how that is so, it's important to understand some things about how your mind works.

But first, some facts about the history of hypnosis . . .

FACT: Hypnosis is older than recorded history. Thousands of years ago, primitive peoples in Africa and Australia used chanting, drums, and the fixation of their eyes to achieve the state we now know as hypnosis. They were able to effortlessly perform amazing physical feats and easily endure situations that would ordinarily cause excruciating physical pain.

FACT: For 200 years scientists, physicians, surgeons, theorists, and researchers have been using and studying what we now call hypnosis.

FACT: What we now call hypnosis originated with an eighteenth-century Austrian healer, Franz Anton Mesmer (1734–1815), who hypothesized that the magnetic pull of the heavenly bodies influences the human body. This theory was called *animal magnetism*, and later, *mesmerism*. Mesmer's methods were theatrical and profoundly unconventional. For example, the venue for his treatments was a darkened hall, where the patient was virtually submerged in a water-filled oak tub with objects such as broken glass, iron filings, and empty bottles placed inside. The tub's cover was pierced with iron rods, which the patient would wave over the diseased parts of his body. Although Mesmer produced astounding results and healed many people without medicine or surgery, mesmerism was widely criticized. Mesmer was soon associated with the occult and accused of flagrant charlatanism because his experiments blended astrology and metaphysics in a way that was not appreciated at the time. (His thesis at the University of Vienna, where he studied theology and medicine, was entitled, "The Influence of the Planets on the Human Body.") He didn't get the approval of the scientific community, yet his efforts were not for naught. None other than Benjamin Franklin, the American ambassador to France at the time, was on the committee that investigated him, and Franklin thought Mesmer's claims and abilities were worthy of further consideration.

FACT: In the early 1800s several pioneering Frenchmen continued investigating and experimenting with mesmerism. Eventually, in 1843, it was a well-respected English surgeon, James Braid (1795–1860), who coined the term "hypnotism" and differentiated it from mesmerism. Braid demonstrated that hypnosis was a state that could be easily induced by the fixing of the patient's eyes on a single object.

FACT: Hypnosis was successfully used as anesthesia for thousands of operations before chloroform and ether were discovered and later (and slowly) accepted for use during surgery.

FACT: Hypnotism was widely used by physicians and psychologists during World War I and World War II to treat battle fatigue and mental disorders resulting from war.

FACT: The British Medical Association and the Council on Mental Health of the American Medical Association have unanimously endorsed hypnosis.

FACT: Hypnosis is now frequently used in medicine, dentistry, and psychotherapy. It is used as a part of the treatment of psychiatric/psychological disorders, the effects of incest, rape and physical abuse, allergies, anxiety and stress management, asthma, bed-wetting, depression, sports and athletic performance, excessive self-consciousness, smoking cessation, obesity and weight control, sleep disorders, high blood pressure, sexual dysfunctions, concentration, and test anxiety.

Modern Hypnosis

By far, the most influential figure in modern hypnosis is thought to be Dr. Milton H. Erickson (1901–1980), the founding president of the American Society of Clinical Hypnosis, who had degrees in both medicine and psychology. Erickson used myriad verbal stratagems and guided imageries to help his patients access their own inner abilities to heal themselves and optimize their performance in many areas of their lives. One of Erickson's most profound contributions was that the subconscious can be indirectly accessed to promote healing. In other words, when he was hypnotizing his patients, he didn't tell them *what* they were feeling ("you are getting sleepy"). Instead, he suggested to them that they *might consider* feeling a certain way ("perhaps you might notice that you are feeling sleepy"). Milton was able to put someone into a deep trance in a short period of time without mentioning the word "hypnosis" at all.

This might not seem to be a big difference, but it is, because it puts patients in a position of personal control and freedom. They have their free will and can choose whether to, for instance, get sleepy. When we feel a sense of control, relaxing and accessing the subconscious is easier and more likely to occur.

Erickson also pioneered the use of verbal strategies that are very closely related to Neuro-Linguistic Programming (NLP—to be discussed in the next chapter). He realized that the way the mind processes certain words, combinations of words, words with multiple meanings, and even pauses and longer silences, profoundly affects what the mind thinks and what the body does. This will become clear in the next chapter, but for now, understand that Erickson demonstrated that language is an extraordinarily persuasive tool. It can engender positive/negative change, it can increase/decrease performance, it can increase/decrease physical and mental pain, and it can even help an individual to consciously control bodily functions that are usually not under our control (e.g., your heart rate).

Erickson was at the forefront of clinical study and research that demonstrated that the unconscious can be responsible for many of our psychological problems and dysfunctional behavior. He amassed a group of zealous followers dedicated to furthering his work and, when he passed away in 1980, those followers started schools of applied psychology based on his work.

As we'll see in the next chapter, Neuro-Linguistic Programming (NLP) is one of those schools of applied psychology that is influenced by the Ericksonian model of hypnosis and hypnotherapy.

At the beginning of this section, I stated that Erickson is thought to be the most influential figure in modern hypnosis. That's because there is another figure who, in my opinion, is just as influential, yet rarely gets the credit he is due. His name is Dave Elman (1900–1967), and he was not a physician or psychologist. In fact, he had no medical training whatsoever; he was a musician and radio producer. And he was a self-taught expert in hypnosis who began sharing his expertise—primarily with physicians, surgeons, and psychiatrists—in the late 1940s. Some say that Milton Erickson learned much of what he later would be known for from Dave Elman.

The Brain and the Mind: Where the Action Is

The brain and the mind have different jobs. In order to understand how hypnosis works, you need to understand what is occurring inside your head as you use self-hypnosis to achieve peak performance.

The Brain

The brain is a tangible thing. It's about three pounds, it has about 30 billion (yes, with a "b") neurons, and it's spongy. You know where it is and roughly what it looks like. It has properties that dictate how it functions, and we know what those properties are. One of them, the one that is most important for hypnosis, is the brainwave.

The level that our brain is operating in dictates how we feel, how we behave, and how we perform. The hypnotic state is attained by taking your brain from beta, which it is probably in right now, to either the alpha state or the theta state, depending on how deeply you need to go for what you'd like to achieve. There has been much research into the four levels of electrical activity that emanate from our brains in the form of brainwaves. Here's a brief review of (or introduction to) the brainwaves and what occurs at each of the four states of consciousness . . .

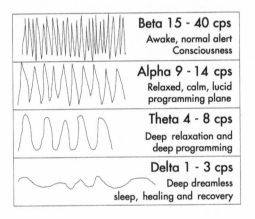

BETA

- ■ It's the center for logic, analyzing, and reasoning.
- ■ In beta, you are awake, normal, and alert. This state of consciousness is characterized by sense-experiences: sight, sound, smell, taste, and touch.
- ■ When measuring this state of consciousness on an EEG (electroencephalogram) or other biofeedback machine, we find that it registers at 15 to 40 cycles per second. That's fast.
- ■ At its maximum capacity, beta comprises only 12 percent of your total being. Relying on beta is like relying on your motorcycle to pull your double-decker motor home.
- ■ The high level of brain activity in beta significantly affects the brain's ability to: store information (memory), access creativity, focus, and concentrate on the workings of the physical body.
- ■ You spend about 90 percent of the day with your brain in the beta level, but when you get stuck here, tension and negative thinking

usually result. And the more stressed you feel, the faster your brain will go, and the less likely you are to achieve alpha, which is where you'd rather be. You'll see glimpses of where you can go and what you can do, but they will be fleeting.

ALPHA

- Alpha is the strongest, most prominent brain rhythm.
- Alpha is the optimal state for your brain when preparing for competition.
- When measuring this state of consciousness on a biofeedback machine, we find that its frequency registers at 9 to 14 cycles per second.
- The brain's biochemistry is completely balanced in alpha and the brain functions at optimal level.
- Decision-making is at its peak in alpha.
- This level is necessary in order to achieve behavior modification. In alpha, you are relaxed, calm, and lucid. This is the programming plane, where you can add new programs and delete old ones. You can also control your dreams while here.
- This is where you are during that first 20 minutes when you are falling asleep, but not quite asleep.

THETA

- Theta is where you are after that first 20 minutes when you were falling asleep, and before you are sleeping deeply.
- Active dreaming takes place here.
- This is the level achieved when you are being hypnotized by someone else, such as during hypnotherapy or stage hypnosis (in other words, it is very difficult to attain through self-hypnosis). This is where you can create hallucinations, amnesia, and physical perception changes.
- Deep programming takes place in theta.
- Theta is characterized by deep relaxation and clear mental imagery. This is where you aim to go when you meditate. You can also experience painless surgery, dentistry, and childbirth in theta.
- Brainwave frequency is measured at 4 to 8 cycles per second.

- In theta, tasks are so automatic that you are not consciously aware of what you are doing (like when you drive home and have no recollection of the actual drive).

DELTA

- Delta is deep, dreamless sleep. The body is completely at rest.
- This is where healing and recovery take place.
- The brain operates at 1 to 3 cycles per second. That's really, really slow.

The Mind

Although the mind isn't something you can point to or describe, there are some things we can say about it. Perhaps the most important conclusion many scientists have reached in the twenty-first century is that if all of the organs of the body produce the same chemicals as the brain when it is thinking, the mind comprises the entire body. The mind's location isn't restricted to the brain; hence, the mind-body connection.

The easiest way to understand the mind, for the sake of a discussion about hypnosis, is to think of yourself as having basically two minds: your conscious mind and your subconscious mind. Your conscious mind is your thinking, awake state of awareness, yet it comprises a remarkably paltry 12 percent of your mind. Let's see what's in that 12 percent . . .

Your Conscious Mind

Your conscious mind has *five functions*.

1. Analytical
2. Rational
3. Willpower
4. Working memory
5. Voluntary body functions

Conscious

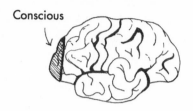

1. ANALYTICAL

First, your conscious mind is logical because it is your *analytical mind.* Its job is to analyze problems that you have and figure out how to handle them. This comes in handy when you are balancing your checkbook.

2. RATIONAL

There is also a *rational part* of your conscious mind. The function of the rational part of your conscious mind is to give you reasons why you do the things you do. Did you ever notice that you can always come up with logical, sensible reasons for why you do the things you do? We call this "rationalization." The only problem with this rational reasoning is that even though it's logical, 99 percent of the time it's incorrect. This is because the true motivation for our behavior and responses comes from a deeper part of the mind that we just don't have easy access to with the conscious mind.

This rational function is important because it allows you to conjure up answers to some very difficult questions. For instance, have you ever asked a smoker why he or she smokes? Your smoker friend might say something like: "I smoke because it relaxes me and gives me time to pause and gather my thoughts." Even though this isn't the true reason a smoker smokes, it sounds rational and logical and the smoker can comfortably continue to smoke.

Note that the rational function is also the *rationalization* function, which means it creates lies when you need them (like what your smoker friend says). The sole job of the conscious mind is to think and provide judgments. And part of its job is to protect the feelings felt by the subconscious mind, which means it will LIE to protect the subconscious. Another excellent example of this function is when a rider says, "I fell off because my horse was spooked." Meanwhile, the real reason for falling off was that the rider was nervous and looking down at the ground. The rider's reason, while not true, sounds rational and logical, and allows the rider to not accept responsibility or feel at fault.

3. WILLPOWER

The next part of conscious mind is the part that you ask to do things that it was never really meant to do: this is your *willpower*. Willpower is your ability to control your behavior by stopping and thinking about that behavior first. If you stop and think about what you're going to say and do before you say or do it, then you are using your willpower.

Willpower doesn't work very well for changing habits because it's tiring to consciously think before you act for an extended period of time. The moment you let up, the habit comes right back! All of us have tried using willpower to change something that we dislike about our riding. Before coming to see me many of my clients tried to use willpower to change bad habits, such as looking down before their jumps or riding with too long of a rein, but they weren't successful. They all had the same result: a temporary success, followed by a rebound right back to the habit they were trying to extinguish. And sometimes that habit is even worse on the rebound.

4. WORKING MEMORY

The *working memory*, or short-term memory, is the only memory you need to get through life on a daily basis. Once a bit of memory no longer serves a useful purpose, it just seems to disappear and we seem to forget it (although we don't actually forget it). And this is the way it should be. We shouldn't have to remember everything we've experienced, all of the time. That would just clutter up our minds too much.

5. VOLUNTARY BODY FUNCTIONS

You can stand when you want to, sit when you want to, and raise your hand when you want to because your conscious mind is able to send messages to what we call your *outer shell*. Your outer shell is composed of the large muscles controlled by the conscious mind. The inner core of your body is the purview of the subconscious mind and includes functions such as breathing, heart rate, new cell growth, and digestion. This distinction is important because if I asked you to control your digestion, could you do it? I submit that you can, but only by accessing your subconscious through some form of hypnosis.

Perhaps the most important thing to remember about the conscious mind is that it accounts for only 12 percent of your entire mind! If you're thinking that the really important stuff happens elsewhere, you're right . . .

Your Subconscious Mind

The subconscious mind is a level of awareness that you generally don't have easy access to in a waking state, yet it represents a whopping 88 percent of your consciousness! Your subconscious has some features that might surprise you . . .

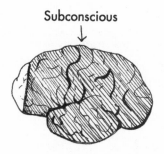

Subconscious
↓

IT'S THE BOSS

Authority means power, right? Well, it probably won't surprise you to discover that there is no power in the conscious mind's 12 percent. That little boss goes through life shouting, talking a mile a minute, thinking, thinking, thinking, providing color and drive—but it has no power of its own.

The subconscious, on the other hand, is quiet like the night sky or the deep of the ocean. Its single most significant characteristic is that it deals from unawareness. It's completely blind. It doesn't tell you, "Say boss, I picked up some info for you." No, it goes quietly about its business performing all its functions. It is so vast and yet so totally ignored as part of your mentality. In fact, most people go through their entire lives ignoring that it even exists. Meanwhile, with only the small 12 percent working for them, they wonder why life is so difficult.

Like an iceberg, the human mind shows only its tip. The rest is hidden out of sight—quiet, dark, and ever obedient.

How do we know we have this much power?
Any time the human body is traumatized, the power within is revealed.

> Exhibit A: We've all heard stories such as this one: A boy jacks up the car and it falls on him. His 100-pound mother lifts the car several feet off the ground, for several seconds, while her son rolls to safety. Where did she get the power and energy?

> Exhibit B: It was said that when her husband was shot, Jackie Kennedy took enough Amytal (a muscle relaxant) to flatten a platoon of men, yet remained awake for three days and nights, completely overriding the effects of the drug. How?

Exhibit C: Your riding and jumping are flawless and you consistently experience peak performance, without ever thinking about it. How?

We can allow the mind to function as it was meant to function when we discover how it operates. Reaching the subconscious requires no effort, no concentration. It's a matter of allowing, not forcing. You allow yourself to relax and then you are in the most receptive state of consciousness.

The subconscious cannot think or reason, and it cannot argue.

It can't judge the merit of an idea, either. But it can do something very powerful. It tells you whether something is smooth or rough, hot or cold, sad or funny, and painful or pleasurable. It feels.

The subconscious is your emotional mind.

You have feelings about everything in your life but, most of the time, these emotions are beneath your conscious awareness, in your subconscious mind. Ordinarily, whenever something triggers an emotion, the subconscious opens up so that you can feel that emotion consciously. As human beings, we all get to experience the full range of emotions, and that can't be helped. You learn emotions in different ways. Not all are learned by direct experience; some are learned by watching them. Either way, they live in your subconscious, so that if you need to change them you now know where to find them.

Who you are, how you respond, and what you believe are functions of your subconscious mind.

All of your automatic responses come from your subconscious mind, including your beliefs. You don't have to stop and figure out what you believe to be true in order to respond to a situation. You simply know what you believe to be true and your responses are based on those beliefs.

Your habits are a function of your subconscious mind.

When you do the same thing in the same way, with enough repetition the subconscious mind will make it a habit. A habit is an automatic response, or reminder to respond, to a certain situation in a specific way. For example, you probably have a habit of mounting your horse from his left side. Each time you approach your horse, you immediately go to his left side. Why? Because your subconscious reminds you to. Why? Because that's what you've always done. Why? Because that's what you were taught way back when. Why? I don't know, but I do it, too.

Approaching your horse from his left side is a neutral habit—it doesn't hurt your riding or help it. Some habits are positive, though. I have a client who checks the girth before getting on his horse as he prepares to mount. He has done it so many times that merely approaching the horse triggers an automatic response. He has used his subconscious mind to create a habit that serves him.

As we all have experienced, there are also habits that hurt us. For instance, people who call themselves "social smokers" will find themselves unconsciously picking up a cigarette when they order a drink or walk into a bar—simply because that's what they've done so many times and because they will be the first ones to tell you that they aren't smokers, they are *just* social smokers. Their subconscious minds corroborate that idea by creating the behavior to support it. Luckily, any habit can be changed by working with the subconscious mind through hypnosis (even the habit of calling yourself a social smoker and the habit of smoking).

The subconscious mind stores the memory of not only everything you experience, but also all of your thoughts, fantasies, daydreams, and night dreams.

This occurs because *your subconscious mind cannot tell the difference between something that is actually happening to you and something that you are imagining.* The subconscious mind records everything you experience, whether real or imaginary, as a memory, and reacts to both with the same intensity. Your inner mind cannot tell the difference! Hypnosis uses that concept to help you reprogram your behavior. Many hypnosis techniques use the imagination to help you actually change what your subconscious is thinking and feeling.

(Note that because of the subjective nature of long-term memory, we never assume that a memory recalled in hypnosis was something that actually happened. We may address it in hypnosis *as if* it really happened, but we would never assume that it had.)

The subconscious protects you from real danger and imagined danger.

An important aspect of your subconscious mind is your protective or self-preserving mind. Its job is to protect you against danger, both real and imagined. This is how phobias or irrational fears can develop. The subconscious mind is using a powerful emotion called "fear" to try to protect you from what it believes to be dangerous. For example, if a car swerves in front of you, your subconscious will jump to action and tell you to swerve to avoid it. That reflex, and the adrenalin that courses through you and that odd, butterfly-type feeling that instantly materializes in your stomach, come from your subconscious.

The subconscious houses your imagination.

All of us were born with this marvelous faculty we call "imagination." It seems like every child has more than his share. Almost immediately teachers, parents, and other well-meaning adults attempt to turn it off. We must learn to deal with—and in— "reality," they say. To many people, however, reality means worry, anxiety, hard work, and no fun. And to them, I say, what if everyone in the world turned off his imagination? We would never have anything new. As you may have heard or read, Thomas Edison failed three thousand times when working on the light bulb. He had every reason to give up. Yet, it has been written that much of the fodder for his continued experimentation arose out of catnaps. The images are the tools the subconscious mind uses to explore and communicate and hypothesize.

Just remember that in the same way the imagination can help you reach your goals, it can also prevent you from reaching them. Many of the difficulties you experience in your life probably originate in your imagination. And they are so powerful that your mind transforms them into your reality. Once again, your 88 percent overrides your 12 percent.

How the Conscious and the Subconscious Work Together

The subconscious and the conscious minds complement each other; they work together, each doing separate tasks. Your subconscious registers your feelings and impressions, and promptly passes them on to the conscious, at which time they register in your awareness.

The only thing the subconscious can do is agree with you; it was designed by nature to be your servant. If you say, "I'm a terrible jumper," your subconscious will produce exactly what you tell it to produce. It cannot say no to you.

Think of the mind as operating like a computer. The conscious mind is like the desktop on the display.

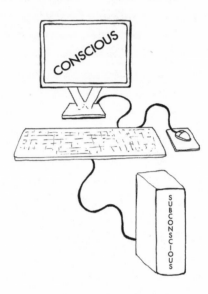

Picture the desktop: What's there? The icons for files you're dealing with right now, and the ones you can easily access with the click of a mouse. Meanwhile, your subconscious mind is like the hard drive that stores all of your files. Where the heck are they, anyway? Unless you're a computer expert, all you know is that *they're in there somewhere, and they've got all my stuff!* And you also know that without their programs, your information would just be mumbo jumbo.

Regardless of whether you believe your hard drive was empty when you were born or was already filled with thoughts and memories from lives past, it can still be reprogrammed.

Little by little, your hard drive has been programmed by your life experience so that today you are a sum total of everything that has ever happened to you. And I mean everything—from impressions of everything you have ever done, seen, heard, tasted, smelled, or imagined.

Everything?

Yes, because your subconscious holds your long-term memory (sometimes called "permanent memory"). Recall that I mentioned that you seem to have forgotten some things from your past. The key word there is *seem*. In reality, you have never forgotten anything that has ever happened to you. Every impression is stored somewhere in your subconscious mind. Using certain hypnotherapy techniques, you can recall or re-experience early childhood events, even your birth experiences.

With hypnosis, you can also change your attitudes and beliefs and thereby change your emotional responses. It's possible to reduce guilt, anger, hatred, and resentment, which opens you up to experience other emotions such as care, joy, and happiness. Who wouldn't want more of those?

You can even strengthen your memory because deep relaxation brings harmony and close rapport between your conscious and subconscious and makes it easier for them to cooperate. In a state of hypnosis, they work together swimmingly and seamlessly.

How to Observe Your Subconscious in Action

Because this may be your initial exposure to an altered state of consciousness, and in order to give yourself every opportunity to observe your subconscious mind in action, the following exercise will illustrate that:

1. You do have a subconscious mind.
2. It does operate effortlessly.
3. You can guide and utilize its powers.
4. You can tap it for information.

Memory Exercise

- As you retire for the night, make yourself as comfortable as possible.
- Close your eyes and relax.
- Ask yourself a question to which you have temporarily forgotten the answer. It can pertain to anything:
  a. the name of an old friend
  b. a long-forgotten teacher
  c. an old address

    d. a phone number

    e. a word in a foreign language that you learned but cannot
       recall. (Be specific and also be sure that you once knew the
       information you are requesting. It has to be in there some-
       where in order for you to access it. This isn't about creating;
       it's about locating.)

- Then, command that sometime during the next day you will have a revelatory thought about your question—that you will suddenly find the answer in your mind and recognize it as the answer.

- Just as soon as you've asked your question and have set the stage for receiving the answer, forget about it and quietly go to sleep. Your subconscious will unfailingly give you the answer to your question if you let it. The same applies for the next day. Stay occupied and don't let your mind wander back on the question—and certainly don't obsess over it. Your subconscious cannot function as directed if your conscious mind is constantly interfering.

- When you least expect it, the answer will appear.

Let's review the properties of the conscious mind and the subconscious mind:

Conscious Mind	Subconscious Mind
12 percent	88 percent
Master	Servant
Effect	Cause
Thinking	Feeling
Perception	Blindness
Awareness	Involuntary
Will	Power
Activity	Quiet
Light	Darkness
Objective	Subjective

Hypnosis is simply about making a change in the subconscious mind. This is very powerful because if a suggestion is allowed to go into your subconscious mind, then it has the power to change your beliefs and change your behaviors. So how does a suggestion get into your subconscious? In other words, how does hypnosis happen?

The Critical Factor of the Conscious Mind

There is another part of the mind that operates automatically when you are using your conscious mind. Dave Elman called it the "critical factor" of the conscious mind, and it acts as a critic or a judge of all suggestions presented to you. Its job is to protect the status quo of your beliefs in your subconscious mind. This is an important function because if you didn't have it, anyone could walk up to you, say something, and totally manipulate you. When you hear a suggestion, your critical factor checks with your subconscious mind to see if that suggestion is in agreement with your existing beliefs. If it is, the suggestion is allowed to go into your subconscious and the belief is made stronger. If it isn't, the suggestion is rejected and there is no change.

You can really see the critical factor in action when you try to discuss religion or politics with someone who has beliefs different from yours. Because the critical factor doesn't allow the opposing belief to enter the subconscious, you keep steadfast to your own. So how do we get suggestions into that subconscious mind? How can we effect change of belief and habits?

We use hypnosis.

Hypnosis bypasses the critical factor of the conscious mind in order to open the door to your subconscious mind (i.e., your hard drive) and focus the mind to accept positive information, such as suggestions. In other words, a hypnotist is a kind of human computer reprogrammer. If an idea is permitted to enter into your subconscious, you are positioned to change. In fact, you will automatically begin to respond differently.

In hypnosis we push the conscious mind aside. Adults have a very hardcore critical faculty made up of all of the facts and figures and nonsense they have picked up all through the years. This critical faculty will leap to the defense of any preconditioned idea and instantly refute it. So let's say an overweight woman is lying on the couch—not in alpha, just lying there. Let's say I tell this individual: "You are slender." She will get up and say, "Are you out of your mind? I look in the mirror and I can see what I am. I'm fat!" Do you hear what she is putting into her subconscious mind?

In alpha and theta, however, there's just no way the woman can struggle to fight the idea of being thin. She'll just drift off while the "You are slender" idea goes right into her subconscious mind. It'll bypass her critical factor and grow stronger and stronger as it is reapplied over and over. Eventually, the notion of thin is stronger than the notion of fat and *poof,* she manifests thin physically because her subconscious mind says that's what's real.

Why a Hypnotist Can't Control You

Now if this was all there was to hypnosis, we hypnotists would be able to control our clients. All hypnotists would be millionaires, and we'd all be thin, for sure. But since we know that's not the case, I want to address the one element to hypnosis that prevents a hypnotist from being able to control you: you never lose the awareness of the suggestions given to you.

Yes, when you enter hypnosis the critical factor is bypassed, but now your conscious mind takes on the important job of protecting you against suggestions that are not good for you or that you don't wholeheartedly want. You see, when you're in hypnosis, you can hear perfectly everything that's going on. Actually, all of your five senses become sharper and more powerful. Your state of awareness is heightened and your ability to decide what you will and won't do, or what you will or won't accept, is much stronger when you're in hypnosis. So you see, your conscious mind is still aware and you can hear every suggestion that is given to you.

> The Critical Factor works for and protects the subconscious mind but resides in the conscious mind. Hypnosis is the bypassing of the Critical Factor of the conscious mind and the establishment of acceptable selective thinking.

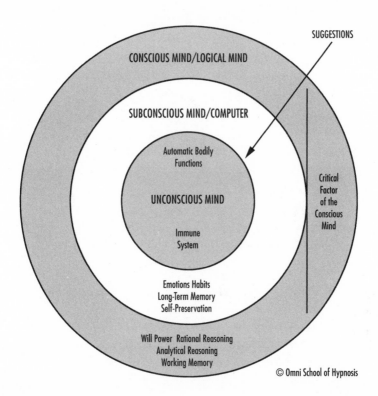

© Omni School of Hypnosis

Our subconscious mind is where our brain deals with habits, emotions, long-term memory, and self-preservation. It is the part of the mind that the hypnotist focuses on, and the part through which it is possible to bypass the conscious mind entirely in order to open the door to positive change.

You've Already Been Hypnotized Hundreds of Times

A hypnotic state (also called a trance) is a natural state of mind. Believe it or not, you go in and out of hypnotic trances all day long. You'd be surprised just how many times your critical factor is being bypassed every day. For example, we've all heard of "highway hypnosis." That's when you're driving down the road and you don't remember driving the last block or maybe the last several miles or perhaps you missed your turn.

That's because while you were daydreaming, your subconscious mind took over driving for your own protection.

Television is one of our greatest hypnotizers.

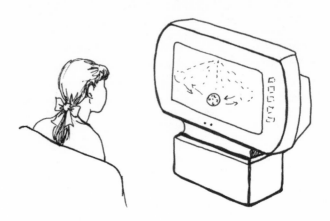

We tend to zone out and get very relaxed while watching TV. So much so, that sometimes we even ignore things going on around us. Add to that the fact that advertisers know everything hypnotists know about bypassing your critical factor. Advertisers use that knowledge to suggest to you or to hypnotize you into buying their products. Branding experts, in particular, use the principles of hypnosis to persuade you that you simply must acquire the *feeling* that the brand will give you: that you must buy their products because you can't be happy or whole without them. Think of how mindlessly you walk through a department store, directly to the brand—the designer—whose clothes you ordinarily buy. Why?

Authority figures can also bypass your critical factors. For example, you will tend to believe people you look up to: those whom you think know more than you do. This includes doctors, schoolteachers, preachers, and motivational speakers. All kinds of people bypass your critical factor. Anytime you're feeling a strong emotion such as love or fear, anger or grief, you are more suggestible. Things said to you, or things you say to yourself, will bypass your critical factor and become part of your subconscious programming. So you see, you don't have to be in any kind of relaxed state at all to accept suggestion. You don't even need to close your eyes. We call this "waking hypnosis," and it happens every day.

Hypnosis Can Extinguish Fears and Phobias

Phobias, extreme anxiety, some fears, and excessive behaviors can all be extinguished through hypnosis, although they require more than just the average positive suggestions to impact them significantly. We don't develop phobias out of a habit, but rather because of some situation that profoundly frightened us in the past. Usually, this situation occurred during early childhood, yet we continue to relive it—and even exaggerate it. For example, most people have a fear of public speaking to some degree and many people are terrified of snakes, spiders, flying, or heights. We learn these fears from early experiences sometimes long forgotten. With hypnotherapy techniques, you can remove your fear by changing the response where it lives in the subconscious mind.

But you have to have the right attitude . . .

Attitude Is Everything

Three mental attitudes affect your hypnotic state. The mental attitude you hold when you hear a suggestion determines whether it goes into your internal computer in order for change to begin, or whether it's rejected and there will be no change.

1. The first mental attitude you can hold onto when you hear a suggestion is: "Boy I like that suggestion. I know that that's going to work beautifully for me!" Yes, and it will. This attitude means that you passionately want and trust the suggestion, and it should be allowed into your subconscious mind. And because the suggestion is allowed to go into your subconscious computer, the change happens.

    The other two mental attitudes will cause you to reject the suggestion, and there will be no change at all. They are:

2. If you're thinking: "I don't know, there's just something a little uncomfortable about that suggestion," you will reject suggestions for

change of things you feel strongly about, such as your morals or religion. In short, there will be no change.

3. Finally, you can also be neutral. For example, you don't care if you get it or you don't get it, but you're willing to try new things. Unfortunately, there's just not enough energy behind that suggestion for it to make much of an impression, so it's rejected, and there is no change. If you've ever heard someone say something like, "I tried hypnosis and it didn't work," that's because they've probably held on to this last mental attitude and caused their own failure in hypnosis. When they heard a suggestion, they said to themselves, "I like that suggestion. I sure *hope* it works." What they didn't realize was that hope means doubt, and doubt rejects the suggestion. (There's much more about words and how your subconscious interprets them later.)

If you hope it's going to work, you really don't believe it's going to work and, therefore, you instruct your own mind to reject the suggestion. You can hope all day long that I'm going to make you change and it simply won't happen. I cannot control you. But if you want the change and you focus on the suggestion with a positive attitude, trusting that it will work, the suggestion will be allowed in and positive change will definitely happen!

Don't be neutral. Embrace the mental attitude that says, "By golly, I like that suggestion, and I know it's going to work for me." When you do that, hypnosis can make changes happen so easily it seems like magic. So you see, you are the one in control: you determine whether or not you can change with hypnosis. When you allow your hypnotist to bypass your critical factor and introduce the suggestions you want, you will get the change you desire.

Remember:

- The hypnotist cannot control you, make you do things you don't want to do, or make you tell secrets. You are always in control.
- Hypnosis is a voluntary act. You can only be hypnotized if you want to go into hypnosis and are willing to follow the hypnotist's instructions. When you do this, nothing can keep you from going into hypnosis. Everyone can be hypnotized if they want to be.
- You are not asleep or unconscious during hypnosis; you are always aware and able to hear, to talk, and to make decisions. In fact, you are in a state of heightened awareness. You experience hypnotic trances, without intent, several times a day.
- Hypnosis can create powerful positive changes in your life when you hold a positive mental attitude toward a suggestion offered to your subconscious mind.

Hypnosis is an especially powerful instrument of change when it is paired with Neuro-Linguistic Programming, as we'll discuss next . . .

CHAPTER 2

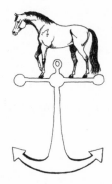

NEURO-LINGUISTIC PROGRAMMING:
What It Is, How It Works, and Why You Need It

FACT: NLP (Neuro-Linguistic Programming) is used by millions of people around the world in a variety of fields including sports, business, education, therapy, and personal development (think Anthony Robbins).

FACT: NLP was first developed in California in the early 1970s.

FACT: There isn't one, definitive version of the history of NLP that all of the parties involved agree on.

FACT: One thing everyone does agree on is that two twenty-somethings at the University of California at Santa Cruz started NLP. Richard Bandler, a psychology student, and John Grinder, an associate professor of linguistics, began studying the thinking and behavioral skills used by particularly effective and successful people.

Two of the successful people Bandler and Grinder studied were Virginia Satir (who is considered the mother of Family Therapy) and Fritz Perls (who was the founder of Gestalt Therapy). Bandler and Grinder were able to distill down the thoughts and behaviors that they felt were largely responsible for the success of Satir, Perls, and the others they studied, and they presented their findings in workshops.

FACT: Bandler and Grinder were introduced to the work of Milton Erickson, and began pondering hypnotic techniques in addition to their growing (and by then diverse) body of knowledge about effectiveness and success that they called NLP. Their initial target audience was therapists and they published books, facilitated seminars and workshops, and produced a cadre of students, some of whom went on to start their own NLP centers.

FACT: By the early 1980s, Bandler and Grinder went their separate ways. But NLP kept growing and diversifying, with an increasingly strong presence in the UK. It was officially becoming a movement.

So what exactly is NLP anyway?

NLP has been called an owner's manual for your brain. It has also been called the study of excellence, the study of success, and the science of achievement. And all of that is accurate. NLP is a practical explanation of how to succeed. It is based on observable phenomena, not theories. And it works. Most important, it's simple . . .

- ■ NLP examines success for its underlying patterns of thought, belief, and behavior.
- ■ Then it seeks to reproduce the thoughts, beliefs, and behaviors that create success, thereby reproducing success.

And when I refer to success, I mean in communication, in relationships, in work, and in riding. Success in life.

When you become knowledgeable and, more important, skilled, in the techniques of NLP, you will be able to:

- Learn new things faster than before.
- Master what you can already do well.
- Manage your emotions more effectively.
- Think more clearly.
- Concentrate better.
- Achieve peak performance in riding.
- Enjoy riding more than ever before.

Sounds appealing, doesn't it?

Let's Get Started!

Please note that much of NLP pertains to communicating and relating better with other people. Although that part of NLP is fascinating and has been highly successful, I am going to focus on the part that pertains to achievement and can help you on your way to peak performance. We'll begin with the most frequently asked questions.

What exactly does NLP mean?

The name is the result of attempting to describe exactly what Grinder and Bandler were doing.

N = Neuro, referring to the mind (and particularly its connection to the body)

L = Linguistic, referring to the potential for change using language

P = Programming, meaning the study of patterns that create success and failure, and programming yourself with the success patterns

Why do I need to learn about it?

- Because it'll improve your performance—and your life—in a short period of time.
- Because it's probably the easiest thing you can do to improve your riding.
- Because it has been working for three decades.
- Because we all need all the help we can get.

Why Learning About NLP Isn't Enough

If you want to produce any kind of lasting change in your behavior—including your performance—the decision to change is your first step. Then comes learning whatever it is you need to learn to create your change. And then comes the most important part: practice.

I constantly hear people saying things like, "I'm going to get better at my transitions this year" or "This is the year I'm going to overcome my fear of crashing."

What keeps many people from accomplishing these types of goals is simple. What do you do if your trainer teaches you how to make better transitions? You practice it until you get it right, of course. What eludes most people is that changing the way we approach things mentally happens the same way. So if you feel like you beat yourself up over past mistakes and you want to change that behavior, you'll be much more successful if you practice, practice, practice.

The bottom line is that we ought to learn from past mistakes and make adjustments in future behavior. The strategy of berating yourself for past conduct solves nothing and only serves to lower your self-esteem. You create a vicious cycle where negative experiences and negative feelings are reinforced, which leads to more negative outcomes and more negative feelings.

Practicing what you learn from NLP is a great technique for improving your performance, but if you really want to put yourself on the fast track to peak performance, you need to retrain your brain using hypnosis, as well. Hypnosis and NLP are like eating well and exercising: you'll lose weight if you do them separately, but when you do them together, you'll lose more weight, faster. You'll turbocharge your weight loss.

The Essentials of NLP

NLP's most popular saying is: *If you always do what you've always done, you'll always get what you've always got.*

NLP techniques set out to alter our verbal and nonverbal communication so that we produce the results and reactions we intend to produce. There are plenty of books on NLP in your local library and your local bookstore, and there are several Web sites dedicated to it. And while there are some subtle and not-so-subtle differences in interpretations of NLP and its use, there are also some essentials that everyone agrees on.

Here is a set of essential principles of NLP, which we call *presuppositions*. No matter who you are, what kind of horse you ride, or how long you've been riding, these will be true.

Everything You Do Sends a Message

Think about it. Everything someone else can see, hear, or feel, that is coming from you, is communicating *something* about what you are thinking and feeling. From body language to eye movement to tone of voice to the speed of your breath and the pace of your speech. We all communicate virtually all the time—even to our horses—we can't help it.

Some of the things that come from you that affect others are in your control, and others don't appear to be. Emotions, for instance, begin internally. Then they produce physiological changes that occur in the human body that tend to produce predictable outer manifestations of those emotions. Here are a few examples of this phenomenon.

ANGER

When you are angry your heart and breathing rates jump, your blood flows to your hands in preparation to hit something, and your overall energy increases. The volume and projection of your voice also increase, in order to attempt to instill fear in anyone who is threatening to you.

When Jessica gets angry, she takes it out on her horse. She jerks on his mouth, kicks him hard with spurs, or she beats him with her crop.

FEAR

When you feel fear, your heart and breathing speed go up, but your blood takes a different direction; it leaves your face and surges to your legs for a quick escape (the flight portion of "fight or flight"—see above for the fight part). Momentarily, your body freezes, making it possible to determine if hiding would be better than running. The volume and projection of your voice lessen to minimize the potential of drawing attention to yourself.

Mark notices that he becomes "like a noodle" when he is afraid. He is loose and limp and easily thrown because he is not committed to his position.

DISGUST

Disgust is usually indicated by the shunning of your senses. For instance, your eyes squint, your face turns away, your lips curl, and your nose wrinkles. Your vocalization becomes staccato and is marked by quick, short outbursts of breath, similar to what you do when you spit out unwanted food.

Brianna's pony kept missing his leads, and she became very frustrated. She was stiff and negative, and her facial expression clearly showed her feelings.

LOVE

Love is a relaxed state marked by increasing blood flow to the lips and hands accompanied by an open physical bearing and deep breathing, which facilitate contentment and cooperation. Vocalization becomes more resonant, perhaps to soothe and charm.

After working with the self-hypnosis CD for Basic Relaxation, she reached the point that as soon as she grasped her leads, she became relaxed and focused on what she was doing.

■ You can usually tell what message has been received because people—and even horses—will respond in a way that tells you what message they have received.

■ There are no mistakes in outcome.

If you haven't been as successful as you would like, chances are you have developed patterns of thoughts and feelings that have left little room for any other outcome. In fact, if you are regularly successful at anything, chances are you have developed patterns of thoughts and feelings that have left little room for any other outcome.

In other words, with a few exceptions, there are no flukes when it comes to outcome. Every failure—and every success—has a clear path that leads to it. NLP is about examining the clear paths to success and creating similar paths so you can reproduce success. NLP has the tools to help you create your path.

We are all products of patterns that we have created—consciously and unconsciously—for our entire lives. Nothing about us is because of chance.

That can be good, as we may have developed patterns that serve us: that work for us. But it can also be bad, as we have unwittingly developed patterns that are destructive, or at best unproductive.

■ There is no such thing as failure in NLP; there is only feedback.

If the feedback you have isn't what you wanted, you should change what you did in order to change the feedback. In other words, if what you're doing is not getting the results or outcome you desire, you ought to change what you're doing.

■ You can create a list of behaviors that work and don't work—in your own life.

If you work backwards from your successes and your failures, you can list what you did that caused the outcome. That's NLP: a set of descriptions about what works and what doesn't. There is no judgment about good and bad; there's simply what works and what doesn't work.

■ It's easier to change yourself than it is to change anyone else—and that includes your horse!

■ The map is not the territory.

Though you have an intention behind your communication, that intention is meaningless unless it matches the message that those around you receive. In other words, *the map is not the territory*—meaning our perception is what creates our reality. NLP is about altering your perceptions, as they are what define what you call "reality." Similarly, your memory is not an exact replication of what has occurred in the past; it is your perception, your visual representation of past occurrences.

■ What you think is what you get.

There are four mental-conditioning laws for the conscious mind that I have found are particularly helpful to my clients:

1. You are what you concentrate on.
2. What you concentrate on seems real (because real and imagined cannot be discerned).
3. What you concentrate on grows.
4. You always find what you concentrate on.

■ You don't know what you don't know.

In NLP's model of learning, we call this *unconscious incompetence*. Experts/coaches/therapists/hypnotherapists are helpful because you don't know what you don't know. But once you do, you are at the point of choice. Then, you know what you don't know, and you can choose to do something about it.

In NLP, when we achieve peak performance, excellence, or personal best, we say that we have evolved from . . .

unconscious incompetence → conscious incompetence →
conscious competence → unconscious competence

Think of it this way, unconscious incompetence is how you started riding: you didn't know what you didn't know. Then you learned about just how much you didn't know. You reached a state of conscious incompetence.

After some training and practicing, you become aware of what you are doing to be successful. You have reached the state of conscious competence. And finally, you reach a state where you are no longer aware of thinking about what you are doing to achieve success. This is your ultimate goal, and it is called "unconscious competence."

■ You can change the way you communicate.

With some education and training, you can control your emotions and their corresponding physical manifestations. That will take some time, and although it is possible if you dedicate yourself to it, in order to achieve success you will need *feedback*, as that is what tells you how you are progressing (or if you are progressing).

If you try to change your behavior all by yourself, you can go off in the wrong direction and never know it. That's why you need feedback.

When you combine NLP with hypnosis, you create the opportunity to speed up and deepen the changes you want to create. This powerful combo puts you on the fast track to excellence!

■ The fastest way toward peak performance is to find someone who already exhibits it and do what he or she does.

NLP uses several techniques to produce and reproduce excellence. The ones I use most in my practice are:

- Modeling
- Circle of Excellence
- Theater of the Mind
- Anchoring

Modeling

The theory of Modeling says that we can achieve excellence in anything by finding a place where it already exists and copying the traits and behaviors present when excellence is present.

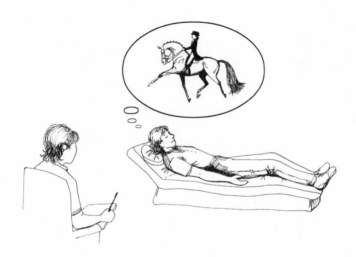

Things to Do:

- Imagine someone riding with ease, poise, confidence . . . excellence. Keep that picture in your mind for a moment.
- Look at the person's body position, from the tip of her feet to the top of her head. Memorize it. Put yourself in that position.
- What are you thinking about that allows you to be in that position? What are you feeling?

These are the thoughts and feelings you want to develop. This is modeling.

Meanwhile, back in your real life . . .

When you are on your horse what do you ordinarily think about? What do you feel? What ordinarily occurs?

- Are you thinking about work?
- Are you thinking about the last conversation you had with your spouse?
- Are you thinking about how you are going to lose weight?

When you think about anything other than the peak performance you expect, don't be surprised when your performance doesn't measure up. What you think is what you get.

Circle of Excellence

The Circle of Excellence is the people and images, sights and sounds, you surround yourself with that are indicative of excellence, and that exude excellence.

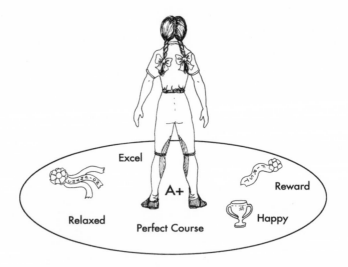

Picture yourself in the middle of a circle, and then fill that circle with whatever has contributed to your excellence and whatever is proof of your excellence. Accessing that mental image—and its corresponding confidence and self-esteem—re-creates that excellence. Remember, the subconscious mind responds as if that circle is your reality.

Note that when NLP refers to excellence and what has caused it, it's referring to what we can directly observe as the cause of excellence. This isn't about theorizing about what actions *might* have resulted in or contributed to a state of excellence. This is about cause and effect. What people, actions, places, and processes have contributed to your success? Visualize them and place them in your circle.

Theater of the Mind

> With real-life practice, some moves will be done excellently, but others less well. With mental practice, however, it is possible to repeat, in your mind, time after time, a move that you remember doing in the past. If the original move was really good, the imagined ones will be just as good. It seems that this repeated imagined activity stimulates nerve connections in the brain in the same way that real activities do. This sets up pathways for repeated excellence and, because there will be no errors in your mental activity, the repeated movements will enhance the skill when put into practice in real life—often more so than real-life practice.
>
> —Carol Harris, *NLP Made Easy*

If you're thinking that Theater of the Mind is characterized by visualization, you're correct. We must recognize the power of our imaginations; it is 88 percent of our minds! The better you are at using your imagination, the more successful you'll be when you use Theater of the Mind later. Here's how it works:

- You are making a movie of yourself. You're the director and you're also the star (what could be better?). We've all done this a million times and, since the advent of music videos, most of us put music to our movies, as well.
- Whenever you are called upon to use Theater of the Mind, you'll create the entire scene. What do you look like, who's around you, what's around you, what kind of day is it, what are you wearing, and what does your horse look like will all be a part of your movie. The object is to create as realistic a vision as possible of the outcome you'd like to achieve.
- Add as much sensory information as you can pack into your movie. It's 3-D, it's scratch and sniff, and you can even taste it.
- Remember to also add internal dialogue. In movies, there are voiceovers to tell us what the characters are thinking. What are your characters thinking? What are they feeling?

Here are some tips for enriching Theater of the Mind experiences:

- Learn to control your imagination. Practice visualizing. Imagine that your hands are lighter and lighter and your feet are heavier and heavier. It might sound like hocus-pocus, but if you can master these exercises, that means you can affect your body with your mind. That skill is highly desirable—in fact vital—to success using Theater of the Mind and hypnosis.
- Learn to use your imagination when preparing for constructive activities, such as riding. The next time you are preparing to ride, pay close attention to everything around you. Attend to things you usually take for granted, such as your gait, your posture, and everything about your horse. Although these details may seem like minutiae, they will be helpful later when you are creating one of your Theater of the Mind productions.
- Develop your creativity. Visualize new inventions, new services, new movies, new approaches to riding.

- When your perception tells you that you're up against a wall, let your imagination run wild. Brainstorm. Don't judge your ideas or edit them—just let them flow and associate freely.
- Practice and practice and practice until you are comfortable using your imagination easily and effectively.

Anchoring

Anchoring is a technique that creates a response through the use of association. It's based on classical behavioral conditioning and involves creating a trigger that will be connected to a desired response. It completely bypasses your conscious and creates an instant reaction. The conscious mind can't stop the reaction you have programmed.

Anchors can be just about anything: a touch (e.g., when you take the reins), a sight (e.g., when you see the ring you're about to show in), or a complex set of movements (e.g., when you mount your horse). The key is to attach the anchor to a desired emotional response. For example: *when you take the reins, you immediately relax.* I have found that anchoring is the tool that creates the most powerful, lasting changes in my clients. I use it multiple times in all of my personal sessions and all of my CDs, and I recommend that you get comfortable with it and use it when you create self-hypnosis scripts of your own.

Know Thyself!

NLP will help you immensely in your daily performance because it is a vehicle for self-knowledge. The more you know about yourself, the better you'll be able to plan your transformation and growth (yes, you can plan your personal growth, and I'll show you how in Part IV).

Once you know, from observation, how others look at the world, you are in a better position to effectively and efficiently communicate with them, as well. Furthermore, the more you know about other people, the better position you are in to predict their behavior. Think about it: You have two friends who are similar in a lot of ways and share many of the same interests. For instance, they both like to ski. One, however, prefers moguls while the other prefers cross-country skiing. Who do you think needs more stimulation?

Perhaps the most helpful aspect of NLP for hypnosis and self-hypnosis is to understand which sense is the dominant one you prefer to use when taking in and processing new information. Research has shown that most people are **visual, auditory,** or **kinesthetic** (and far fewer are gustatory or olfactory). Here are some quick tips on how to determine which one you are:

Visual people (55 percent of the population) tend to focus on pictures, colors, sizes, angles, contrasts of focus, and brightness. They tend to talk fast, think in pictures and charts, and prefer to be *shown* how to do new things. They often speak of how they "see" things ("Looks good to me." "I see what you mean." "The future is looking brighter."). They pay careful attention to their appearance and the appearance of others. Their respiration is shallow and quick. They use words such as:

- Appear
- Clarity
- Display
- Emerge
- Focus
- Hindsight
- Illusion
- Look
- Notice
- Peek
- Peer
- Probe
- Scene
- See eye-to-eye
- Sketchy
- Stare
- View
- Watch
- Witness

Auditory people (21 percent) focus on words, volume, cadence, inflection, pauses, pitch, and tempo. They are good at handling people, are open to both sides of an argument, and like good questions. They think in language, talk about how things sound ("Sounds good to me." "This rings a bell." "I'm all ears.") and are dominators of conversations. Background noises can either bug them or help them. If you want them to do something, you should explain it to them (not show them or give them written instructions). They breathe deeply and speak rhythmically. They use words such as:

- Announce
- Boisterous
- Confess
- Deafening
- Echo
- Growl
- Howl
- Mention

- Outspoken
- Resonate
- Screech
- Speechless
- Tongue-tied
- Utter
- Vocal
- Whisper

Kinesthetic people (24 percent) focus on feelings, texture, vibration, intensity, pressure, tension, and movement. What they perceive is often a reflection of their feelings. They are touchers and they judge situations and people by how they make them feel inside ("That doesn't feel right to me." "She's so thin-skinned." "I have to dig deep for the answer." "She's all washed up."). They breathe deeply and slowly, are more patient than the other types, and they speak lower and more slowly. Because they take most of their cues from their feelings, they are more prone to moodiness. They use words such as:

- Burning
- Caress
- Euphoric
- Firm
- Heated
- Lukewarm
- Muddled
- Pressure
- Relax

- Rush
- Shift
- Solid
- Stress
- Stroke
- Touch
- Unsettled
- Whipped

Things to Do:

If you're still unsure of which category you fit into, try this: write a story about one of your fondest memories. A couple of paragraphs is usually all that is necessary. Aside from reliving an enjoyable moment, you'll be able to determine which of your faculties you tend to see your world through. Examine your choice of words. Which sense appears to be dominant in your story?

This will come in handy later when you create affirmations and self-hypnosis scripts for yourself because their effectiveness is contingent upon how specifically and intensely they appeal to the lens you use to process new information.

Hypnosis and NLP are powerful tools when used properly and together. In the next chapter, I'll introduce "laws" that dictate why and how things happen the way they do in our lives. When you factor these laws into the retraining of your brain, you can create meaningful change in any area of life you choose.

CHAPTER 3

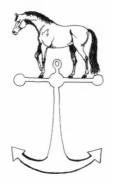

THE LAWS OF THE UNIVERSE
and the Natural Laws of the Mind

My mentor, Dorothy Gates, taught me the following laws. They have much in common with philosophical and spiritual traditions of the East, and have been increasingly accepted in the West. Some of them had the dubious distinction of being introduced during the New Age movement, but we have since amassed plenty of evidence that they are valid, and not as whimsical, nonscientific, and "out there" as they were once considered to be.

Laws of the Universe
The Law of Cause and Effect

It is the eternal law of nature that there can be no effect without a cause. Things do not just happen. They come into being and are the results of our thoughts, actions, and deeds. In terms of your mind, that means that your results are the 12 percent, but the causes represent 88 percent of your mind. So everything has a cause: you just might not know what that cause is.

As Dr. Gates used to say, "If we make mistakes in life, we eventually pay the price. We are the arbiters of our own destiny." She frequently used the metaphor of the harvest. "Thoughts we dwell upon in our minds are the seeds, and the seeds will create an entire harvest according to the law of 'like produces like.' All seeds must reproduce according to type. Seed determines the type; harvest reveals the seed sown." *Whatsoever a man soweth—that shall he also reap.* Perhaps this Biblical quotation will take on new meaning for you now.

Our world is busy applying Band-Aids to the effects of our "problems" when we should be doing major surgery on their root causes: the causes that can be found within each individual. Wisdom is the faculty of knowing what will be the effect of a cause.

Every action in the universe must be followed by an appropriate reaction. There is no exception of any kind, at any time, for any reason. We will get out of life what we put into life—no more and no less.

The Law of Free Thought

We learn to remain (of our own free will) within the natural laws of our being. All things ideal must exist in us before they can exist in society. Peace, plenty, and security are not detached from us; they are not things that exist apart from us. Unless we learn these basic laws of nature, we will remain ignorant of the most important thing of all: how to conduct our lives so that we might richly live. We are rich or poor, happy or sad, depending upon how effectively we use the laws of our natures. We can choose to use our free thought and free will for good or not, and we will always face the consequences of our choices: sooner or later.

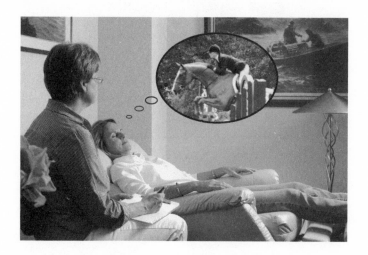

We are, in fact, the sum total of our choices.

—Dr. Levy in Woody Allen's
Crimes and Misdemeanors

The Law of Work

We live in two spheres: vocational and personal. The wise person seeks to achieve harmony between the two. Our purpose is to make a contribution while we are here as creative beings and to advance the act of living to some degree by having lived. We should all be occupied in the highest employment of which our nature is capable, and leave this life with the consciousness that we have done our best. No one can ask more of you than that you do your best.

The Law of Human Relations

Everything stems from the individual; society is an extension of the individual. The first human unit is the individual, then the family, the community, the city, the nation, and the world. The contribution of every nation is the result of the quality of its citizens. Everyone cannot sit around waiting for another fellow to start doing something to improve society. YOU are the starting point. I am the starting point.

We owe it to ourselves and to each other to do what we can to promote peace and compassion. Remember that one warped mind affects everyone in the community. We've seen that time after time.

As Dr. Wayne Dyer writes in *The Power of Intention*, "Be the peace you're seeking from others . . . see the light in others, and treat them as if that is all you see." If you need love, be love. If you need compassion, be compassion. Whatever it is you want from this life, be that first. And because like attracts like, you will attract what you need once you have *become* it.

The Law of Perception

It is impossible for any of us to be objective about our own lives. Every human being is the exact center of his own life and the way he thinks and feels has a direct and all-powerful influence upon the way in which he interacts with others as well as his environment. We see our world not as IT IS, but as WE ARE. Whatever happens or occurs is treated subjectively always.

Best-selling author Richard Carlson, Ph.D. discusses precisely this in *You Can Be Happy No Matter What: Five Principles for Keeping Life in Perspective.*

> We have innocently learned to interpret our thoughts as if they were "reality," but thought is merely an ability that we have—we are the ones who produce the thoughts. It's easy to believe that because we think something, the object of our thinking (the content) represents reality.

The Law of the Eternal Present

The subconscious is geared to act, react, and respond in only one time period—NOW—the present. Everything it does and everything it can do, it does now. The future is nothing more than your present expectation of an incident or event yet to take place. You anticipate or plan for tomorrow—NOW.

As Eckhart Tolle writes in his best seller *The Power of Now: A Guide to Spiritual Enlightenment*, "Nothing exists outside the now."

> What you think of as the past is a memory trace, stored in the mind, of a former Now. When you remember the past, you reactivate a memory trace—and you do so now. The future is an imagined Now, a projection of the mind. When the future

comes, it comes as the Now. When you think about the future, you do it now. Past and future obviously have no reality of their own.

The Law of Change

Life is filled with changes. It's whether we can cope with those changes or not that determines whether we will grow with the situation or be overcome by it . . .

—Joan Borysenko, Ph.D.,
Minding the Body, Mending the Mind

Our creativity and efficiency is directly commensurate with our appetite for change. Inability to adapt to change signals atrophy in this natural appetite with the result being indecision, doubt, fear, and dullness. Meanwhile, change stimulates the magnificent creative faculty of the subconscious. And though none of us knows what is ahead, all things pass away and all things change; the important thing is to use today wisely and well and face tomorrow eagerly and cheerfully.

We are not just passive victims of our ever-changing world, however. We can create change if we desire to. In Louise L. Hay's classic book, *You Can Heal Your Life*, she discusses the process of change. "When we have some pattern buried deeply within us, we must become aware of it in order to heal the condition," she writes. The next step is to "acknowledge our responsibility in having created the situation or condition . . . and [allow] yourself to learn what you need to learn."

Once you have acknowledged the past and learned from it, it is time to release the past and forgive whomever you believe has injured you. And that includes forgiving yourself. I use a technique called Release and Clear, which I'll outline later. As Hay writes:

The only thing you ever have any control over is your current thought. . . . Your old thoughts are gone; there is nothing you can do about them except live out the experiences they caused. Your current thought, the one you are thinking right now, is totally under your control.

In other words, you are in complete control over if, when, and to what extent you will change. The power lies within you in your thoughts. You can use your thoughts to decide to change and then to create a new behavior that you can eventually transform into a habit.

The secret of handling our changing conditions
is adapting to the Natural Laws of the Mind.

Natural Laws of the Mind

Law 1: What You Think Is What You Get

Any image placed into the subconscious mind develops into reality with absolute accuracy. Life is not determined by outward acts or circumstances; it is formed from the inside out. Each of us creates our own life with our thoughts. A single thought will neither make nor break a life; a habit of thought will. You cannot think defeat and be victorious.

The subconscious mind responds only to mental images. It does not matter if the image is self-induced or from the external world. The mental image formed becomes the blueprint, and the subconscious mind uses every means at its disposal to carry out the plan. Worrying is the programming of an image you don't want. The subconscious, not knowing the difference between a real or imagined image, acts to fulfill the imagined situation and "the things I feared most have happened."

As Wayne Dyer writes in *Manifest Your Destiny*:

> If your mental pictures are of being surrounded by things and conditions that you desire, and they are rooted in joy and faith, your creative thoughts will attract these surroundings and conditions into your life. . . . What you are doing is literally visualizing in detail what it is that you want to manifest. . . . You detach from the outcome and how it will be accomplished. You are not in the business of creating, but of attracting to yourself what is already in creation . . .

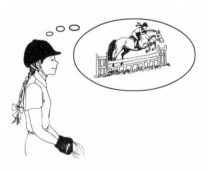 

When you change your thoughts, you change your mind.

Law 2: Every Thought Causes a Physical Reaction

Our power of creation is the word. The word is the most powerful tool that humans possess. It is the tool of magic.

—Don Miguel Ruiz,
The Four Agreements Companion Book

Your thoughts affect all of the functions of your body. Worry thoughts trigger changes in the stomach that eventually lead to ulcers. Anger thoughts stimulate your adrenal glands and the increased adrenaline in the bloodstream causes many other physical changes. Anxiety and fear thoughts change your pulse rate. Hunger and thirst thoughts affect your stomach and salivary glands. Sex thoughts affect your sex organs.

Our personal body chemistry is guided and triggered by our emotions. Thought, however, leads the emotions. You can make yourself sick, poor, and unhappy by your habitual thinking. Many people don't realize that it is a law that you become what you dwell upon. The law of electricity must be obeyed before it can become man's servant. When handled ignorantly, it becomes man's deadly foe. Just so with nature's laws.

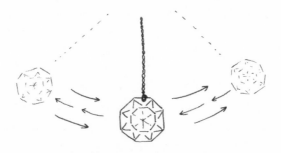

The best way to instantly grasp Law 2 is The Lemon Test. Read the following a couple of times until you have committed the short process to memory. Then, close your eyes and see what happens!

Imagine you are in your kitchen on a bright, sunny day. Look around you and notice the colors and the light in the room.

Slowly work your way to the refrigerator, noticing everything along the way. Notice which way the door to the refrigerator opens. When you open the door, you notice a lemon on the shelf in front of you. Look at a lemon. Feel it. Pick it up, bring it to a cutting board next to the sink, and pick up the sharp knife lying next to the cutting board. Slice the bright, yellow lemon in half. Picture yourself smelling the lemon, bringing it to your mouth, and then squeezing some of the juice onto your tongue.

Did you salivate? Did your mouth pucker?

Law 3: Imagination Is More Powerful Than Knowledge

Images are the property of the subconscious mind (that huge 88 percent of you we discussed in Chapter 1). Those images will always overpower what you think (the scant 12 percent). Reason is easily overruled by imagination. In fact, an idea accompanied by a strong emotion usually cannot be modified through the use of reason. By subconscious reprogramming, however, any idea can be easily and effortlessly removed, altered, or amended.

The way I teach my clients about this Natural Law of the Mind I say, "Look at me right now. I am wearing a red shirt and khaki trousers, right?" then, "Okay, now close your eyes and picture me with a green shirt and purple trousers and a black hat."

Now open your eyes and tell me which is real.

Your mind doesn't know, as it has seen both and cannot tell the difference.

Law 4: Your Habits Are Your Life

Sounds dramatic, right? But think about it: life is full of habits. Much of your day consists of successions of actions that have become more or less automatic. Ninety-eight percent of what we do, we do by habit, spontaneously. Each separate act (habit), good or bad, plays a part in making you what you are. Fortunately, it's never too late, and you're never too old, to change your habits. You can begin today. You can begin right now, at this very moment. Remember that success is a habit and failure is also a habit. Repetition forms positive habits and negative ones.

Men do little from reason, much from passion, most from habit.

YOU CAN FORETELL YOUR FUTURE

A surefire way to tell what your future will hold is to look at your habits of today. If you don't change any of your habits of today, there is one place they will inevitably lead you.

For example: If you have a habit of always hanging your head and looking down ("having a bad eye"), you will leave little time to make decisions about adjusting your horse's stride. You also won't have a good sense of rhythm and speed. And if you do nothing about your habit of looking down, I can guarantee you that your sense of rhythm and speed will not improve.

If you want to change your habits, you have to work at it.

Extinguishing bad habits involves cultivating new ones. And that work has to be on the subconscious level. If you could change by just reading a book about change or going to therapy, everyone would be replacing all of their negative thoughts and behaviors with positive ones. But it's not that easy. Reading doesn't create change easily or automatically. You need something more.

One of the things you need is repetition. What you use increases; what you don't use, or abuse, will atrophy from lack of use. All of your talents increase or decrease in proportion to the extent to which you apply them. Once a habit is formed, it becomes easier and easier to follow and more difficult to break.

Napoleon Hill refers to "The Three Essentials of Cosmic Habitforce" in *Keys to Success: The 17 Principles of Personal Achievement.* What he's really talking about is how and why we form habits. The first essential is "plasticity," which is simply the ability to change that is part of our makeup. The second is "frequency of impression," which means that the more you do something the faster it becomes a habit. "Repetition is the mother of habit," Hill writes.

Finally, "intensity of impression" is the third essential and means that the greater the concentration involved in doing something, the faster it will become a habit. "You impress the habit on your subconscious mind, and it becomes a part of everything you do."

Make good habits and they will make you.

Law 5: Don't Breed Negative Thoughts

As you probably have learned through experience, the more attention and power you give to your fears, the more they affect you and the more likely they are to manifest themselves. If you continue to fear ill health, constantly talk about your "nerves," "tension headaches" and "nervous stomach," in time those organic changes will occur. Your nerves will act up, you'll get tension headaches, and you will experience stomach problems. All because you kept those negative notions in your mind.

This is true with any negative thought. The more you concentrate on missing your jumps, the more likely you are to miss your jumps. In general, the more you allow fear and other negative thoughts to invade your life, the stronger their presence will become. And once they are firmly entrenched in your mind, your body will begin to create behavior to support them.

Law 6: Attitude is a Matter of Choice

You cannot control the external circumstances of your life, but you can control your reactions to them.

—Joan Borysenko, Ph.D.,
Minding the Body, Mending the Mind

An attitude is basically the way in which you look at life, and as we have all experienced, attitudes affect the body and how the body performs. Fortunately, we all have the innate ability to choose our attitude in any given set of circumstances.

The events that occur in our lives are purely neutral. They are not positive until we have decided that they are, and they are not negative until we have decided that they are. I can decide to view a course as positive and challenging, while someone else can choose to see the very same course as negative and confusing. So in NLP, when we refer to "reframing," we are talking about the ability we all have to shift our perspective and, in turn, change our approach and probably change the outcome.

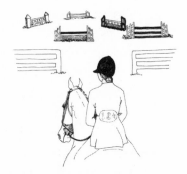

Law 7: Reactions Must Be Managed

This law is the corollary to the previous one. Just as you can manage your attitude, you can manage your reactions. Again, what happens in your life is purely neutral. But how you react to what happens is not; it can affect your health and your performance.

For instance, if you go off course, you have at least two options:

1. Leave
2. Either do your courtesy fence or finish the course

The moment you go off course, you have a decision to make, and that decision will start a chain reaction. If you succumb to your emotions and feelings of defeat, you set yourself up to go in one direction, but if you can manage those feelings and set your sights on the bigger picture, you will go in a different direction.

> *All feelings are good, because their purpose is to provide us with information, direction, and motivation that will help us create a satisfying life.*
>
> —Calvin D. Banyan

Law 8: Thoughts Must Be Kept Alive

No thought is self-sustaining in the mind—it must be nurtured, fed, and kept alive. The first time I heard the sentence: "Only one idea can be entertained at one time," I was thoroughly confused. I was thinking about memory and how we can hold many ideas at once.

But the sentence refers instead to how the conscious mind recognizes an idea as true, correct, and guiding. And that it cannot hold the opposing idea simultaneously. For example, an individual may believe in absolute honesty. He trains and expects his children to be honest. Meanwhile, he cheats on his income taxes. He might rationalize his conduct by saying, "Everybody else does it." He cannot, however, escape the conflict and its effect upon his nervous system that is caused by attempting to hold opposing ideas.

The following are truisms about your thoughts:

- An idea, once accepted, tends to remain until it is replaced by another idea or until it is forgotten.
- Once an idea has been accepted, there is opposition to replacing it with a new idea.
- The longer an idea remains, the more opposition there is to replacing it with a new idea.
- The longer an idea remains, the more it tends to become a fixed habit of thinking. (This is how habits are formed, both good and bad ones: first the thought, then the action.)
- Therefore, if we wish to change our actions, we must begin by changing our thoughts.

Law 9: Attitude of Gratitude

One of the laws of the universe is what you put forth comes back to you—and usually when it does it has gained mass and momentum. In other words, what goes around, comes around. Therefore, if you develop an attitude of gratitude, and you look at your life in terms of all you have to be grateful for, you'll start seeing more to be grateful for, focusing on positive things, and more positive things will then be attracted to you.

In *Manifest Your Destiny* Dr. Wayne Dyer writes, "The nature of gratitude helps dispel the idea that we do not have enough, that we will never have enough, and that we ourselves are not enough. . . . Gratitude is a way of experiencing the world with love rather than judgment."

PART II

THE 6 KEYS TO WINNING FOR THE EQUESTRIAN

CHAPTER 4

BASIC RELAXATION
Your Physical State:
From Tension to Relaxation

Relaxation in this case means more to you than it has in the past. It's about more than letting go of your outer shell, which is controlled by your conscious mind. It's about relieving your inner core, which is controlled by your subconscious mind. It's about releasing tension deep within your body. Deep in your organs, nerves, cells, and spinal column. For many people, this will be the first time they attain such a profound state of relaxation.

The feeling of intense relaxation is enjoyable, but it is also practical; it has a purpose. When you allow yourself to relax, you also allow your subconscious to function without interference from your conscious mind.

That is the state of being that is optimal for accepting suggestions that will create lasting change.

How?

By using hypnosis and the NLP anchors, you can create a change instantaneously. By allowing the anchor to activate, you allow yourself the response of instant relaxation. Better breathing and relaxation produce amazingly smooth communication between your brain and your body. They create the optimal environment for your muscles to do their job, without any competing messages from your brain.

Once you are relaxed, you'll experience the following:

- You'll handle your horse better.
- Your body won't be as tense; your muscles won't be as sore.
- You'll be more aware and alert so learning can take place.
- You'll feel increasingly happy with yourself while allowing that learning to take place.
- You'll feel a sense of peace at being able to effortlessly respond and enjoy the moment.

This chapter will help you develop the art and skill of being able to relax while still feeling comfortably aware, alert, and able to move fluidly.

Tension: Unrest or imbalance, often with
emotional causes and physical manifestation.

Tension affects your breathing (resulting in either hyperventilation or hypoventilation to various degrees), it creates nervous shaking, it can create irregular or extreme energy (lethargy or hyperactivity), and it can even affect your memory.

And all of these negative internal experiences eventually manifest themselves physically, as Natural Law of the Mind 2 says: Every Thought Causes a Physical Reaction.

When you are tense and nervous, the following tends to happen:

- The majority of tension tends to be held in the stomach, causing stiffness in the upper body and sitting up out of the saddle. And when you are sitting up out of the saddle (when you're not supposed to be, such as when you're galloping), you will lose rhythm of your horse's gait.

■ Tension of the stomach also causes tightening of the shoulders, which makes it difficult to feel your horse's movement.

■ Your hands tend to become stiff and clench into fists. Fixed hands lessen your ability to control your horse and yourself because, ironically, you aren't really feeling what you are touching when you are holding on so tightly.

■ Your gaze tends to be downward, which compromises your security and balance.

> *The horse is your mirror.*
>
> —ancient Arab proverb

Remember that your horse takes his cues from you. And this is especially true of your mood and your stance. So if you do not feel relaxed, and your body, as we have seen, will manifest your tension, what kind of message do you think you are sending to your horse?

Notice how Tiffany has a stiff upper body and is pulling on the reins, irritating Lark.

Notice how much more relaxed Tiffany looks. She has a good classical frame and her eyes are up and looking forward.

When you are tense, your horse is likely to be:

- ■ Nervous
- ■ Not manageable or supple
- ■ Rushing
- ■ Not sure which commands he's supposed to be responding to
- ■ Too tense to properly interpret your commands (which are probably not accurate anyway because of your own tension)

All because he is taking his cue from you!

Your ultimate goal is for you to reach the point of unconscious competence discussed in Chapter 2. You want to be so good at what you do that you aren't aware of the specific things you are doing. You want to be comfortable so you can enjoy yourself.

Things to Do:

Take responsibility for your own stress reduction and relaxation. Here are some exercises my clients have found particularly helpful:

Breathe

Find a quiet place and try to empty your mind. Breathe in deeply for five counts, hold your breath for five counts, and then exhale for five counts. Repeat five times. Paying attention to your breath helps block distractions. In fact, some people like to say to themselves, "inhale," "hold," and "exhale," or simply "in" and "out."

Deep breathing → increased relaxation → slower metabolism → muscle tension decreases → brain waves shift from fast beta waves, which occur during your normal waking day, to slower alpha waves, which appear just before falling asleep

Focus Your Attention

Find a quiet place, sit up straight, and focus on an object. Put all of your attention on it while you inhale and exhale, slowly and deeply. When a thought comes into your mind, return to your object of attention. In just a couple of minutes, your tension will diminish, as will your anxiety.

You can also do this exercise by looking at a point on the floor several feet in front of you (so your head is only slightly tilted downward), and blur your focus, so that your eyes are relaxed. Again, when a thought enters your mind, return to your spot on the floor.

Attend to Your Breath

Find a quiet place and sit in an upright position. Breathe deeply and slowly, and be aware of where your breath is most obvious. Is it in your stomach? Your chest? Your nostrils?

Close your eyes and focus all of your attention on your breath.

> **TIP:** The most effective inhale fills the stomach, then the chest, and ends with a slight lift of the shoulders. The breath moves in an upward direction. The exhale should move in the opposite direction: downward. You should exhale slowly, in a controlled manner, until you squeeze the last bit of air out of your stomach.

Add a Word

Next, you can add a word. In most spiritual traditions, there is a word with an "ah" or "oh" sound at the beginning, and an "mm" or "nn" sound at the end. This isn't an accident or a coincidence. These sounds create distinctive vibrations in your head that alter your brain waves and create a more relaxed state. Some examples are "amen," "ohm," and "shalom."

Choose one of the words and repeat it to yourself, both aloud and in your head. The impact is particularly noticeable when you say your word aloud. You'll feel it vibrating in your mouth, face, and head.

Release Muscle Tension

Find a quiet place and lie down with your arms comfortably by your sides, palms up. In yoga, this is what is known as *savasana*, or "corpse pose." Inhale and exhale, slowly, deeply, and completely, ten times.

Bring your attention to the tips of your toes and notice if there is any tension. If not, move up your feet and legs, in search of tension. At each location where there is tension, bring your breath to that point. For example, if your calves are holding tension, visualize the breath from your inhale reaching them and filling them with healthy, cleansing air. Then visualize them contracting, ringing out the air, along with any stress, tension, or pain. To make the experience even richer, add color to this exercise. At each place where you are holding tension, breathe until the tension subsides, then continue scanning your body until you have reached the top of your head and cleared and relaxed each point that was manifesting stress.

TIP: Color is a powerful tool in visualization, as it has been proven to have a dramatic effect on your emotions and your body. You can use color when you are doing your stress management exercises, your relaxation exercises, and your fear-management exercises.

■ Blue is calming and relaxing. It actually physically calms the body, including the pulse rate, breathing, perspiration, and muscle tension.

■ Red is a powerful color that increases vitality, energy, and heat. It can also increase the intensity of the impact of your visualizations. (Note that red placebos are more effective for pain relief than any other color!)

So if you want to calm yourself, visualize your breath as a blue breeze that flows through your body. If you need energy, visualize your breath as a red blaze shooting through your body.

Gail's Story

Because I was so nervous on my horse, I was starting to question my reasons for riding. Thoughts went through my mind like: "Maybe I should start bike riding or running, instead of riding," and "Maybe I should take up tennis with some of my friends." Every time I rode my horse, it seemed like I was just a nervous wreck. Riding was no longer an enjoyable experience for me, and it definitely wasn't something I looked forward to like I once did. It was impossible for me to relax and enjoy the sport. I began asking myself why I chose to keep up this hobby.

I've always thought and always told everyone that I loved horses and that riding was my passion. But the truth is that I don't feel like I am as good at it as I used to be, and it's not as fun for me anymore. I don't succeed at the goals or ideals that I set for myself anymore, and my riding has actually become more of a disappointment for me rather than an accomplishment or an achievement. I have memories of being successful with every horse I ever got on and riding was a great pleasure for me. Enjoying my ride now seems like a far-off, novel idea. Now I dread even going in the barn, and I worry myself sick about how badly I am going to mess up in my lessons.

In the past, when I rode by myself, I used try to jump higher jumps than I did in my lesson or try to really concentrate on what I had just learned. Now when I ride by myself I typically just walk and trot and try not to do anything challenging or new; I take advantage of not having my trainer there to push me to do more difficult things. I keep it very simple, doing only the things I am confident in, just trying to get it over with without a disappointment.

Another thing is that I no longer have the connection with my horse that I used to. That used to be the best part: my mare knowing my mistakes and me knowing her flaws, and we would make up for each other. If I missed my take-off spot for a jump, she would compensate for me. It's like she could read my mind; we were so in tune with each other. I no longer had that with her, and it made it that much more difficult to get the motivation to ride. She had a sore back, and I'm convinced that it was because I was so nervous and tense on her back, that I was the one causing it. I thought that maybe horseback riding was something that I had outgrown. I've always sworn that I would never give up riding. I was strongly considering selling my horse, even though she is a family member to me and I knew it would break my heart. I needed some help, but I didn't know what to do.

A friend suggested I go to a hypnotist . . .

Though I'm extremely skeptical, I was ready to try anything if it might help. I spent a little time checking out the hypnotist who was recommended to me. Her name was Laura, and she looked normal and seemed to be very businesslike. On my first visit I let her know how skeptical I was. It didn't seem to bother her.

She taught me so much and everything made so much sense. Then she hypnotized me. It was really cool. I truly relaxed and enjoyed every part of it. I remembered the whole session and felt really good. She "retrained my brain," as she called it, to respond to several anchors that would trigger my body to feel relaxed and comfortable when I mount and I repeat the word "Relax" several times, silently to myself. When I say this word silently to myself, I feel the release of all my tension. I feel my shoulders relax and my jaw unclenches. When I do mount my horse and once I touch my reins, I feel so much more comfortable than I used to. The reins are an anchor, too. It is truly unbelievable what a little relaxation retraining has done for me.

Now, my rides are more pleasurable because my mare and I are actually working together as a team. I feel more effective than ever before. Since I am relaxed, I am communicating better with my horse. I have noticed that my horse's body soreness has disappeared as well. After I noticed such a difference, I decided that on my next visit to Laura I would narrow in on improving a few of my skills like focus, concentration, and just to be more positive all the way around.

Now, let's teach you how to achieve peak performance through self-hypnosis . . .

> *It is what the subject does, not the operator's wishes*
> *that determine what shall be the hypnotic manifestation*
> —Milton Erickson,
> "Initial Experiments Investigating
> the Nature of Hypnosis"

In Chapter 1, I mentioned James Braid, a surgeon from England who gave hypnosis its name and also helped gain acceptance of hypnosis in the medical community. Dr. Braid was also one of the first proponents of self-hypnosis, and believed that the power of hypnosis came not from the hypnotist, but from the mind of the person being hypnotized. Consequently, anyone who can be hypnotized by someone else, can hypnotize himself or herself. After all, you *allow* someone to hypnotize you—they don't *do* it *to* you.

The crucial element of directing your unconscious is *autosuggestion.* In other words, self-hypnosis is so effective because all of the suggestions for thoughts and behaviors come from the subject (i.e., you!).

As you practice, let your mind and body become increasingly quiet and serene as the mental picture of soothing quiet and peaceful rest unfolds before your imagination. When relaxing, all your inner and outer muscles slacken completely. A feeling of heaviness may develop; then it may change to detachment, lightness, indifference. A new pattern of calm, tranquil living is established.

The Self-Hypnosis Session

Session is another name for the physical act of reaching the subconscious mind. This natural technique is so effective in releasing all muscle and nerve tension within the body that you realize immediately a wonderful sense of well-being and absolute ease. This deep state of rest is accompanied by an improvement in circulation. And your mind, free from tension and useless activity, is able to strengthen and reenergize every muscle, every nerve, and every cell in the body. By releasing deep muscular tension (perhaps for the first time in your life), you alleviate nerve tension automatically. And with freedom from nerve tension comes absolute and complete relaxation.

Relaxation is achieved during the session by means of suggestion. As you relax your mind by letting it dwell upon thoughts of quietness, serenity, and well-being, your body quickly responds to the suggestion of rest by letting go and relaxing. To realize a progressively deeper state of relaxation, all you need to do is maintain this calm, quiet state of mind.

The vital point to remember in attaining the state of deep relaxation? Make absolutely no effort to achieve this state. No concentration or effort is necessary. Simply let it happen.

Effort is the function of the conscious mind. The subconscious mind does everything with ease. It is the subconscious you are working with during your sessions. Since it learns very quickly, your subconscious will soon anticipate what it must do so that with each repetition of the relaxation routine, you will relax faster, more easily, and more deeply.

Rules for Successful Self-Hypnosis Sessions

When you learned to ride, you didn't start out jumping in a Grand Prix. The same is true of reaching an altered state of consciousness. You will first learn a few basic rules and then you must practice, practice, practice. Repetition is your friend. As we say in yoga: repetition is the mother of mastery.

Rule 1: Preset Your Time Limit

■ Ascertain the period of time you desire to relax. Research shows that 20 minutes is the best amount of time. You can, however, use five or ten minutes, depending upon the circumstances.

■ Give your subconscious the command that under no circumstances do you exceed the time limit. Remember, it must obey you. If you find yourself exceeding that time period (especially in the beginning), it may signify that you are releasing a great amount of tension. Only in the beginning and only under extreme stress should you lengthen the time period of practice. If you must, use a clock timer to awaken you until you have trained the subconscious to respond to you. Some of you awaken in the morning without a clock. This works in the same way. Your eyes will pop open, you will have a twitch, or your leg will jump. Something will awaken you. You are seeking a dreamy, detached state (not sleep) wherein you can make clear and definite impressions upon your feeling mind. Total unawareness does not mean sleep. It is merely an indication that you are at a very deep level of alpha.

Rule 2: Get Comfortable

■ Loosen your clothing if it is at all tight or binding. Remove your shoes, your tie, or any article of clothing that may pinch you or be uncomfortable in any way. Position yourself so that the circulation is not restricted. Arms at side, palms up, legs uncrossed, glasses or contacts removed.

Rule 3: Initially Use the Same Place to Practice

■ You will begin to associate the chair, couch, bed, or even floor with the alpha level of consciousness. As you become accustomed to the routine, habit takes over and you will find yourself propelled to that place at approximately the same hour each day. Think of this relaxation period as you would a daily bath—except this is a bath for your mind. If you do your self-hypnosis at work, as well, choose a spot there and form the habit of going to that spot for practice.

■ Don't use your bed if you have difficulty sleeping. Don't use your ex-husband's or ex-wife's chair (there are negative connotations attached to them). Don't practice for at least an hour before bedtime—otherwise you will be alert and awake when you want to sleep.

Rule 4: Use Your Environment

■ Allow every noise, sound, or movement to carry you deeper into the desired state. We live in a noise-filled, busy, active world. To be completely effective you must be able to achieve this state of alpha any time you choose, under any conditions. To do this, simply use your immediate environment to help you relax instead of working to discount it. Prepare for every eventuality. If you are expecting a call, use a telephone to awaken you. If the doorbell should ring, use it to deepen the state. It is up to you to form the habit. Every sound or noise can take you deeper and deeper or it can awaken you. It is your choice.

Rule 5: Always Maintain the Same Attitude

■ Here I go! Expect to thoroughly enjoy this period of relaxation. Assume an attitude. "I relax as deeply as I can go and I enjoy the benefit from the experience." Avoid analyzing, avoid questioning, avoid attempting anything. Simply let it happen.

Automatic Results from Practicing

You sleep better, your mental and physical health improve, and your performance will improve. Without the continual carryover of tension from day to day, your system functions more efficiently. You are more at ease during both your waking and sleeping hours, and you sleep more deeply and more contently, but for a shorter period of time. Twenty minutes in alpha is equal to four hours of natural rest. When you find yourself sleeping less, you will also find yourself with extra hours to do those things you have always wanted to do—extra reading, writing, exercising, or whatever interests you.

Conditioning Yourself to Reach Alpha State

Once you are able to consciously relax your mind and your body, you will be prepared to go into alpha state using the following script. And once in alpha, you will be ready to put yourself into a hypnotic state and accept the suggestions that will lead to changes in your behavior on a deep, subconscious level.

You are probably going to have to practice a handful of times, with the complete script, in order to achieve the alpha state that is necessary for you to accept the direct suggestions in the hypnosis script or CD. You can either read the following script or record yourself reading it (and be prepared to do it a couple of times until you get it right). Note that Basic Relaxation is the only one of the 6 Keys to Peak Performance that includes this version of alpha conditioning. Once you have successfully accessed alpha with this extended script, you'll be ready for Instant Alpha Conditioning, where you access alpha by using a single word of your choice.

Instructions for Alpha Conditioning

1. Practice the alpha-conditioning session for two consecutive weeks, twice a day if possible (most people do it before they go to bed at night). You may want to record it so that you can do it with your eyes closed, which resembles what would happen if I were there with you.
2. Get comfortable. Use the same place to practice and read (or listen to) the section on alpha conditioning. Let it happen.

S	M	T	W	Th	F	Sat

3. After you have had at least 14 alpha-conditioning sessions (I recommend 21), you'll be ready to learn how to access alpha by enlisting the help of a single word. I'll explain how in a moment, but for now, let's begin retraining your brain.

Alpha Conditioning

Under no circumstances do I naturally fall asleep. I allow myself to relax . . . I relax . . . and allow myself to become as comfortable as possible. I feel myself relax. I allow the sensation of gentle rest to begin flowing throughout my body. I can feel myself growing more and more relaxed . . . with each and every breath that I exhale. I visualize a balloon exhausting all its air. I too relax, releasing greater and greater amounts of tension as I exhale . . . dissolving into the deepest state of rest. I feel . . . feel . . . the sensation of soothing relaxation as it begins in my toes . . . and each and every fiber and muscle in each toe . . . now responds to the irresistible urge to let go . . . to let go. Each toe grows limp, loose, and relaxed. As a dry sponge absorbs warm, languid liquid . . . my body absorbs the soothing, languid, glowing quietness . . . of relaxation. Irresistibly . . . the relaxation flows into both my feet. Smoothly, yet quickly, with an ever-increasing sense of pleasure . . . and enjoyment . . . the languid sense of peaceful, calm relaxation reaches my knees . . . and my knees relax. Swiftly now, like that thirsty sponge . . . soaking up warm, languid liquid . . . the relaxation spreads to my upper legs . . . saturating them . . . spreading smoothly into both hips, and I am, from the hips all the way down . . . to the tips of my toes . . . firmly aware . . . and yet deeply relaxed.

With every breath now, my level of conscious awareness grows less . . . and less . . . and less. Feeling safe and secure, my legs seem to fade . . . fade . . . fade away. Every breath is slow and easy . . . slow and easy . . . slow and easy. As I relax deeper and deeper, the same soothing . . . tingling . . . relaxation . . . now begins to develop in my fingertips . . . filling each finger smoothly, deeply, and totally, with the sensation of deep relaxation. Each finger discharges every last bit of muscular tension . . . and in doing so . . . grows limp, loose, and relaxed. As the relaxation grows deep and complete . . . it spills over into both of my hands . . . saturating every tissue . . . every fiber . . . every cell . . . with the most enjoyable sensation . . .

of absolute ease and quietness. As tension is dissipated, I become aware . . . of the sensation of the free-flowing circulation of the blood . . . which adds to the glow of relaxation. Both my hands are now completely relaxed . . . and the relaxation spreads with increasing effectiveness . . . into my wrists . . . and my wrists let go . . . into my forearms . . . and they, too, grow limp and relaxed. My elbows let go as they, too . . . seem to fade . . . fade . . . fade away.

Swiftly now, the glowing sensation of utter calmness and tranquility permeates my upper arms . . . the muscles grow limp and relaxed . . . and finally permeates both shoulders and . . . my shoulders let go . . . very limp, very relaxed. With each soothing, satisfying breath, they seem to fade . . . fade . . . fade . . . from my conscious awareness. My legs are deeply relaxed . . . my arms are deeply relaxed. A soothing . . . penetrating . . . deep quietness of my arms and legs now begins to penetrate, to saturate . . . to fill and to soak . . . the rest of my body . . . with calm, quiet rest. I visualize clear, golden honey flowing smoothly and gently . . . into a clear, glass container. Like the honey, the relaxation spills down from my shoulders, flows down my spinal column . . . bubbling up from my hips . . . and through my body . . . slowly filling with the most pleasant . . . enjoyable sensation of quietness. My back muscles relax . . . my abdomen muscles relax . . . my chest muscles relax . . . and every tissue . . . every organ . . . every gland, deep within my being responds to this soothing sensation . . . by relaxing also. Relax . . . relax . . . relax.

Every sound, every noise, every voice that I hear helps me to relax deeper and deeper. My glands and my organs are smoothly and efficiently . . . growing even more relaxed . . . with each and every beat of my heart. My heart is now pumping soothing . . . easy . . . quietness throughout my being. Slowly and irresistibly now . . . my entire body is filling . . . filling . . . filling . . . with relaxation . . . and soon, my entire body grows limp . . . and then begins to fade . . . fade . . . fade away. As my conscious mind yields to its critical authority . . . as it drifts . . . and dreams . . . and floats . . . the irresistible sensation of relaxation spreads smoothly into the muscles of my neck . . . and each nerve . . . each muscle . . . each fiber . . . grows limp and relaxes . . . responding more and more to the urge to relax . . . deeper and deeper. As my neck muscles relax . . . all congestion is relieved . . . all tension vanishes . . . and the sensation of the most utter contentment fills my mind. My mind urges my relaxed body to let go even more. The soothing quietness spreads into my scalp . . . and my entire scalp lets go.

A blanket of quietness is slowly enveloping my entire being, which I can now feel. I feel a cap of soothing, drowsy rest spreading over my entire scalp . . . and with such ease . . . with such enormous pleasure . . . the languid warmth finally spreads down across my face . . . and every muscle . . . every nerve . . . every fiber in my face grows limp and relaxed. The muscles in my cheeks and jaws let go. I am now completely and totally relaxed. Every breath takes me deeper and deeper. Every breath finds me with less . . . and less conscious awareness, but with greater and greater receptivity of my subconscious mind. I am, from this time forward, growing more relaxed . . . serene . . . and calm during all my waking and sleeping hours. I can, at any time, achieve this same deep sense of relaxation and quietness. I have the ability to relax and I do so . . . with the greatest ease and pleasure . . . making relaxation the easiest thing I do.

Upon awakening . . . I find I am more refreshed . . . and more invigorated . . . than I have ever felt before in my whole life. I always find relaxation refreshing . . . invigorating . . . rejuvenating.

Twenty minutes, wide awake.

Once you have completed the above program, you can progress to a more immediate form of alpha conditioning . . .

Instructions for Instant Alpha Conditioning

Assuming you did the extended alpha script, for 14 to 21 times, under the proper conditions, you should easily be able to progress from the extended script to accessing alpha state by using a single word (you meditators out there will already be familiar with this process, and whatever mantra you currently use will work just fine for our purposes here).

1. Select a word you would like to use to replace the alpha conditioning technique introduced above.
2. Practice this for one week. If alpha state occurs when you use the chosen word, go on with the program. If not, repeat this set of instructions until alpha occurs, using your chosen word. When

alpha consistently occurs, you can use this technique to prepare your mind prior to any of the self-hypnosis scripts.

Instant Alpha Conditioning

From this moment on, each and every time I desire to attain the deep state of total relaxation, I am instantly and fully relaxed, as I am now drifting into the alpha state of consciousness. The moment I think my chosen word _____, alpha occurs. This word has an effect only when I use it and only under the proper circumstances. Each and every time I do use it I am fully prepared to receive positive, beneficial, and constructive suggestions, impressing each one deeper into the storage and memory facility of my brain.

From this moment on, _____ triggers deep relaxation of my mind and body. I feel alpha occur. I feel wonderful. I feel comfortable. I am totally receptive and responsive to my own creative ideas and suggestions. I am bathed in a glow of quietness, peace, and serenity. My chosen word works only when I deliberately use it for deep relaxation to attain alpha consciousness. Its use in regular conversation has no effect on me whatsoever. From this moment on, each and every time I desire the deep state of total relaxation, I am instantly and fully relaxed upon saying _____. Because my subconscious must follow my command, each and every time I desire total relaxation, I am instantly and fully relaxed when I think my chosen word _____. I feel a deep sense of gratification as this word programming becomes a reality. Feeling wonderful, generous, alive, and eager to awaken . . .

Twenty minutes, wide awake.

Once you are able to easily access alpha using your word, your technique will be to:

1. Access alpha using Instant Alpha
2. Proceed to the script for Basic Relaxation, Gaining Concentration, Releasing Performance Anxiety, or whichever of the 6 Keys to Peak Performance you are working on.

The Power of Compounding

At the end of each script you'll notice a sentence that looks something like this:

> This entire suggestion is represented by the letter *R* of my sub-key word, RHYTHM. Anytime I think, say, or see the word RHYTHM, all suggestions keyed to this word are automatically activated, stimulated, and work for my benefit.

Each of the 6 Keys is associated to a letter in RHYTHM. This technique is called "compounding," the effect of which is that each time you see, hear, or say the word RHYTHM, all of the effects of your sessions are triggered and made exponentially more powerful. You need to remember the word RHYTHM at least once every 36 hours to get the full effect.

R	21 sessions of Basic Relaxation
H	21 Sessions of Positive Self-Talk
Y	21 Sessions of Gaining Concentration
T	21 Sessions of Release of Performance Anxiety
H	21 Sessions Fearless Showing and Jumping
M	21 Sessions Peak Performance

After this has all been put into the subconscious mind you will be able to feel the results. Let's begin at the beginning . . .

Basic Relaxation for the Equestrian

When I ride I feel so relaxed . . . I enjoy being with my horse because it makes me feel so good. I feel relaxed when I hold my horse's reins—I automatically feel so comfortable and relaxed when I am holding my horse's reins when I ride. I am able to ride well . . . I am able to be peaceful and alert while I am riding. Because I am calm and relaxed, my horse performs better. I do whatever task I need to do with such confidence, relaxation, and ease. Everything I do comes so easy to me. I find that because I am calm and relaxed on the horse that I am riding that my horse responds to me better. I ride with complete balance ... I handle everything that my horse does with great confidence and self-assurance.

I am very calm and peaceful. I feel great. I completely enjoy the wonderful feeling of being completely relaxed. Relaxation comes to me so easily, so much so that should I try to resist relaxation consciously or subconsciously, my body automatically grows more relaxed. I continue to relax even more soundly and more deeply with every breath that I exhale. I enjoy all these sensations that allow me to relax without any effort whatsoever. My whole body just gives in. The more and more I allow my body to relax, the better I feel. The better I feel, the more and more my body relaxes.

In every way now I feel better, happier, and more content. Every second, every minute, every hour, every day, my self-confidence builds more and more. I have a positive attitude. My mind stays calm and content in all situations. I have the ability to let everything flow in peace and harmony with my new way of enjoying life. I have good thinking and good judgment . . . always relaxed and able to handle all events in my life with the ability to let everything happen in a peaceful content way.

When I ride my horse I feel relaxed and enjoy being on my horse because it makes me feel so good. I ride well because I am peaceful on my horse. I am calm and my horse performs great . . . I do whatever task I need to do with such confidence and ease. Everything I do comes so easy to me. I am calm and relaxed on my horse . . . and my horse responds so well to all of my requests. I feel so comfortable on my horse as I ride with complete balance and ease. I handle everything that my horse does with such confidence.

I feel so marvelous and wonderful every time I ride . . . these wonderful feelings stay with me all the time—every day. I am happy and content when I ride. I give in to the potential of my mind and body. Whatever my mind can conceive, my body can achieve. How great I feel when I am riding . . . how peaceful. All of these suggestions help and guide me to be more and more relaxed every time I ride. I allow my body to relax and to enjoy these wonderful, good feelings that go through my body.

Anytime I desire to feel better than I do, I simply take a moment . . . take a couple of deep breaths, and say the word "relax" quietly to myself. The word "relax" is a conditioned response key to my subconscious mind. When I say this word, I recapture the feelings of being comfortable and relaxed while on my horse. I feel enthusiastic about my future. The word "relax" is my conditioned suggestion. Every time I use my relaxation programming, it becomes more effective. Each time I say the word "relax" while I am on my horse, I ride with harmony, comfort, and relaxation. When I have a lesson or I practice for a show I feel more and more confident. I am in balance and enjoy riding with the rhythm of my horse's gait. I am automatically relaxed when I hold onto my reins. This makes me feel so confident, relaxed, and secure.

This entire suggestion is represented by the letter *R* of my sub-key word, RHYTHM. Anytime I think, say, or see the word RHYTHM, all suggestions keyed to this word are automatically activated, stimulated, and work for my benefit.

Twenty minutes, wide awake.

CHAPTER 5

POSITIVE SELF-TALK
Your Self Talk: From Negative to Empowering

As your own most important critic, it is crucial to your success that you teach yourself to recognize unfair self-criticism and turn it into empowering self-talk. Practicing empowering self-talk and working on your mind-set is actually just as important as practicing the technical aspects of your riding. The same way that the technical aspects of riding (e.g., jumping, lead changes, counter-canters, half passes) need practice, the mental aspects of your riding need practice.

Some of my clients find it extremely helpful to write little reminders, goals, and affirmations on note cards and place these cards where they can see them at the start of the day. If you're having trouble with your mind-set, try making one that says, "I am relaxed and confident every time I get on my horse." Repeat this phrase to yourself often and with a lot of enthusiasm. Before you know it, you'll notice an improvement in your riding performance!

The Little Rider That Could

My clients often express frustration that they possess identical, if not superior, physical attributes to their competition, yet they're consistently being outperformed by that competition. In many of these cases, the factor that separates their performance from the competition is that they are operating with a limiting belief about their athletic abilities and the level of performance they are capable of achieving. Their resulting, flawed performances are evidence that an individual's core beliefs will ultimately determine the reality they manifest.

"I think I can, I think I can, I think I can . . ." said the Little Engine That Could as he chugged up the mountain. More than just a children's story, this is a valuable lesson. *What we tell ourselves has a profound impact on our performance.* In my experience, the single most important and effective thing that all riders can do to improve their performance is to change negative self-talk into positive, empowering self-talk.

> *Whatever the mind can conceive, and believe, it can achieve.*
> —Napoleon Hill,
> *Think and Grow Rich*

Self-Talk Defined

Self-talk is exactly what it sounds like. It's your internal dialogue—the words you use when you talk to yourself either in your own mind or aloud.

Neuroscientists and psychologists have calculated that most people carry on an ongoing dialogue, or self-talk, of between 150 and 300 words per minute. Most of this self-talk consists of the mundane, routine, and harmless thoughts we all have such as "I'm hungry" or "I need to get my hair cut soon."

The danger for riders and other athletes is when this internal dialogue takes on a negative connotation such as, "I'll never be as good as she is" or "I don't even belong riding at this level." When this kind of self-talk becomes ongoing, you create limiting beliefs about yourself and about your abilities that may, if left unchecked, go on to become self-fulfilling prophecies.

For those of you who are academic-minded, consider Expectancy Theory (and the Placebo Effect), which states that you don't always get what you want, or what you work for, but you will more often than not get what you expect. If you expect to miss a fence, you will. If you don't expect to get the ribbon, you won't.

If you think that negative self-talk isn't really that big of a problem in the riding world, check in on any number of equestrian-competition discussion forums on the Internet. You won't need to read long before coming across a fellow rider asking for help with some technique or another while at the same time berating himself constantly and saying things like, "I just can't do it!" or "I must be stupid."

There are many self-talk mistakes that riders commonly make when preparing for and riding in a show, and all of them are easily dealt with, as you'll see in a moment. Among them are:

■ Focusing on the past or future

"I chipped my first three fences last time I was here" or "I can't believe how badly I messed that transition up" are classic examples of not letting go of past mistakes. It's just as counterproductive to worry about what *might* happen. As a rider, you can always have complete control over the present moment, and that's where your thoughts need to be.

■ Thinking only of the outcome

"I need to win" or "I need to impress the judges" are thoughts about the outcome, something that riders have little control over. What you do have control over, however, is performance. Try changing your self-talk to focus on what needs to be done to turn in your best possible performance, and trust that the outcome will take care of itself.

■ Focusing on outside factors beyond your control

"I hate riding when it's humid" or "I never do well when there are so many people watching" are the kinds of thoughts that waste your mental energy and can only hurt your confidence and, therefore, your performance. Work your hardest to keep your thoughts on controllable factors.

■ Focusing on weaknesses during competition

The time to focus on your weaknesses as a rider is during practice or when you're with your trainer. It's necessary during these times to identify where your weaknesses are and then work to improve them. On the other hand, dwelling on weaknesses *during* competition only serves to hurt your confidence and make you more nervous and tentative in the ring.

■ Demanding perfection

Avoid saying to yourself: "This needs to be a perfect go," or berating yourself for small mistakes while in the ring. All athletes make mistakes, but it's the really great athletes who can make a mistake and continue their performance unfazed. It's fine to work towards a perfect go if that's what motivates you, but it's unrealistic to expect to execute the perfect go every time out.

Although I have difficulty with the word "perfect," I have seen perfect performances. And if you've had some performances that were perfect, make sure you use those memories when you are visualizing because that increases the probability that they will recur. "Perfection," however, is a different ball game. Perfection assumes that no matter what you do, there is some other, higher level that you are working toward but that, by definition, you'll never achieve. The idea of perfection makes people drive and strive and exhaust themselves, only to constantly feel inadequate and self-critical.

If you want to demand something of yourself, demand that you do the best you can at each moment.

How to Change Your Self-Talk

Chances are you've experienced a few of the above self-talk mistakes in the past. But how do you actually change your self-talk to be more positive? We can't really control the thoughts that come into our heads, right?

Wrong.

There are two ways to eliminate negative self-talk. One is through a process commonly referred to as *thought-stopping,* which involves four steps:

1. Become aware of self-talk.
2. Stop the negative.
3. Replace with positive.
4. Practice the act of stopping negative thoughts.

Easy enough, right?

The only problem is that for thought-stopping to be effective, it requires lots and lots of practice on the conscious level. The way we think and talk to ourselves can be an extremely hard habit to break, considering we've been doing it a certain way for our entire lives. To improve your self-talk this way, you need to work hard to learn to recognize when you're engaging in negative self-talk, and then you need to work equally hard at stopping those thoughts and replacing them with positive ones. Fortunately, there's an easier, faster way of changing your self-talk.

Lemme guess . . . does it involve hypnosis?

Yes. The second way that you can eliminate your negative self-talk requires very little effort at all because you use your subconscious mind. Your subconscious mind is what tells you that you need to stop at a red light or to pedal the bike to make it go or even to breathe. These are actions that, over time, cease to require conscious thought and seem to happen on their own. In truth, it's your subconscious (which makes up about 88 percent of your mind!) that takes care of these things for you.

Creating Positive Self-Talk

Despite the fact that there are about 750,000 words in the English language, we use only a fraction of them (just a couple thousand, on average). I suggest doing some vocabulary building, and while you're at it, some weeding out as well. There is a handful of words that most people frequently use, which affect the subconscious so negatively that we could all benefit from eliminating them from our vocabularies. Before we discuss what your self-talk should look like, let's first address the most important words to avoid when you're talking to yourself or to anyone else.

Words to Avoid

TRY

Try is one of the most poisonous words in the English language. This venomous little word can cause much misery. *Try* means "to test, to attempt to do something." But its connotation is deadly because it creates three reactions in the subconscious.

1. It programs failure. If at first you don't succeed, try, try . . . again. The ellipses between "try" and "again" means "over and over again." Failure is implicit in the word *try*. I tried to lose weight (but failed). I tried to be a good father (but failed). I tried to remember my course (but failed).

2. *Try* is a wholly negative word. Because life requires a total commitment, and because *try* gives you an ideal out to escape responsibility for doing or not doing something, it is the word many people hide behind. They refuse to commit themselves to yes or no. It's so easy to seek the middle ground and say "I'll try"—whether you want to or not. As you utter the word "try," your subconscious immediately picks it up and says "fail." Listen to people who use the word *try* a lot. Invariably, they are failure-oriented and frustrated.

3. *Try* is not an action word. It doesn't give you anything to do. For instance, you hear the words *sing, run,* and *sit,* and your processor gives you something to do with them. Now do that with *try.* What are you going to do with *try?*

Replace self-defeating talk with "I'll do my best."

HOPE

Every word you speak or hear causes a certain kind of emotional and physical response. *Hope* transmits a subconscious image that promotes a feeling of anxiety—the subtle dread that something bad is about to happen. "I hope I pass the test" creates a negative response. There is an unhealthy feeling and there is serious doubt about what you know or, at the very least, an uncertainty about the outcome of that test. This emotional response takes place without your conscious awareness because our emotions are rooted in the subconscious.

PROBLEM

When you use the word *problem* you are emphasizing an obstacle and generating a feeling of helplessness, which is why this word is so lethal and every self-help guru will tell you to eliminate it from your vocabulary. If you dwell on difficulties, barriers, or defects, the nonselective, subjective mind accepts your thinking as your command and then proceeds to work strenuously to produce the same in your external world. Replace *problem* with something like *challenge*.

CAN'T

> Bobby, age 8: *Mrs. Siegal, can I go to the bathroom?*
> Mrs. Siegal: *I don't know Bobby, can you?*

I remember that same exchange repeated over and over again when I was in grammar school. It was actually a great technique for reminding us kids that *can* means that you physically have the ability to do something. And *can't*, therefore, means that you are physically unable to do something. That is a very powerful, very negative concept.

When you say "can't" you often mean "won't," which implies you have made a conscious decision to opt out. My suggestion is to say what you mean. If you mean, "I choose not to," say so. After all, most people know that when you say "I can't" you really mean "I won't," anyway, and they'll appreciate your honesty.

NOT

Have you ever told yourself, "I will not knock over the first barrel . . . I will not knock over the first barrel . . . I will not knock over the first barrel," and then knocked over the first barrel? We've all repeated similar phrases and had the same outcome: disappointment. Why? Because the subconscious is incapable of producing the word *not* in your behavior. Instead, it produces everything but *not*. So it produces the behavior that supports "I will knock over the first barrel." Need more proof? Quick—do not think of a yellow polar bear sitting next to you. What happened?

Your knowledge of how your subconscious deals with (or doesn't deal with) negative words such as *not, don't,* and *won't,* will be especially useful when you are constructing affirmations for yourself. But as for your daily language, starting today, always state the outcome you desire in the positive, such as, "I am confident in my timing around the barrel."

The Two Most Powerful Words You Can Use

I Am

These three letters, when put together like this—*I am*—are a powerful tool for both negative and positive self-talk. *Why?* Because your subconscious will assume the identity of whatever follows them. Consider "I am so fat" and "I am in great shape." If you were to rearrange those sentences, you'd end up with "So fat, I am." "In great shape, I am." It implies that you and the state of being you describe are inextricable. "You" and "so fat" are the same thing; you are one. So if you are trying to lose weight, you will have a very difficult time because you are carrying around with you the very obstacle you seek to eliminate.

Tips for Improving Your Autosuggestions (i.e., Your Language)

Here are some simple rules to follow when structuring your language—to yourself or to others. You can also use these rules to create affirmations or suggestions when writing your own self-hypnosis script for losing weight, quitting smoking, or whatever else you'd like to accomplish. Remember that your language creates action in the world and that language (both negative and positive) programs your subconscious. And when you're in alpha state, your language will program your subconscious very quickly, and very easily, so as they say, *"Be careful what you wish for . . ."*

1. Be realistic. Though your subconscious mind doesn't recognize the concept of impossible, and will work on anything, there are five areas to avoid, particularly when you are in alpha state.

   a. Avoid working on the mind of another. The one mind you know you can control is your own. Besides, the universe doesn't reward people who try to control the minds of others.

   b. Avoid attempting to change the orderly progression of time.

   c. Avoid thinking you can call upon knowledge, information, and experience you don't have (e.g., you can't fly, you don't have bionic vision or hearing, and if you have no experience jumping, no affirmation or suggestion will make you an instant, perfect jumper).

   d. Avoid the attempt to make physical changes that are impossible (e.g., although some nonhuman animals can re-grow limbs, we cannot. And although I have heard people tell me they used affirmations to increase their bust size, I'm a bit wary of this technique).

   e. Avoid manipulation of that which is beyond your control (e.g., the weather).

2. Phrase everything in the present time. "I will" means later and later never comes. Create a strong mental picture of your objective NOW, and let your subconscious produce it for you.

3. Always use a completely non-resistant (positive) approach. Make no mention of what is bothering you. Create a dynamic and positive image of your objective. Talking about what you don't want

and visualizing what you don't want just makes what you don't want more likely to occur.

4. State your objective clearly. Know exactly what you want. Fuzzy, hazy goals produce little in the way of results. Always work for the strongest possible response—feelings and pictures.

5. Stress activity. You must begin where you are NOW. Stress the activity toward your objective. Visualize your active participation.

6. Visualize. Remember that alpha consciousness responds only to mental images. So when you're in alpha, picture the desired goal as you produce alpha brainwaves. Let the image happen. Thinking is conscious-mind activity, and when you think, you should be restricting yourself to positive, productive thoughts and images.

7. Symbolize. Any concept, goal, or objective that doesn't lend itself easily to visualization can be readily impressed into the subconscious mind by simply assigning a symbol to it. For example, whenever anyone says "horse," an image appears in your consciousness. You then have a feeling of delight, a feeling of anger, a blah feeling, a feeling of excitement—any number of responses are triggered according to your experiences. In this same manner, you can deliberately use words, colors, objects, people, or things to trigger entire affirmations and/or suggestions.

Here are some examples of helpful affirmations that my clients often use:

- I handle stress and tension appropriately and effectively.
- My mood is calm and relaxed.
- I cope well and get on with my life during times of stress.
- My breathing is deep, slow, and calm.
- I am a confident rider.

Sasha's Story

Sasha's story is a great illustration of how you can reprogram yourself to let go of negative memories, clear your mind, and develop a positive, productive internal language that will lead to a better mental state and better performance.

■　■　■

When Laura asked me why I was going to see her, I had no problem responding. I've got a big problem and I know what it is. I tell myself bad things and think bad thoughts. All the time. I could say that I have had some trainers in my past who have contributed to my problem. And it would be true. I still have ingrained in my head things they would say like, "There's no way you'll make that jump" or "You're not good enough of a rider to get the changes in that combination to make it right" or even really horrible things like "Are you even listening to what I'm saying or do you choose to do things the wrong way?" But that's no excuse; I'm a grown-up and I suppose I should just get over it. But for some reason I can't.

I feel especially bad because now I have this great trainer who's really positive and supportive. But as soon as she stops talking to me for a minute, or is silent when I execute my ride by myself, my mind instantly gets negative and critical. And then my performance suffers a lot.

I can't expect my trainer, or anyone else for that matter, to have to talk me through my riding all the time like when I was a small child. I know better than that, but I sometimes feel like a small child who has been told her whole life that she can't do anything right. There is no logical reason for me to feel this way. A couple of bad trainers years ago couldn't possibly create such an effect.

I am a very good and competent rider and have succeeded at many competitions, but it seems that I have become a perfectionist and wish for my riding to be even better. Instead of focusing on the good things and working from them, I always focus on the bad things or my mistakes. Then I end up making a mistake that probably wouldn't have occurred if I hadn't been so worried about it and thought it in my head a dozen times.

The kinds of things that go through my head are: "My horse won't pick up the right lead," "I always clip the last fence in my combinations," and "I'll forget to count my strides." I even have these little movies that play in my head about all of the mistakes I just know I'm going to make.

I know I need to learn to just play out the ideal situation in my mind and focus on the positive and good things about my riding. I know I need to think more about the good things and not so much about the bad things, but it is almost impossible for me to do. I have consciously tried, on several occasions, but it never works for me. I even catch myself riding with my head down sometimes, which definitely inhibits the communication between me and my horse. I've tried to be excited about the small victories and focus on them, like flawless lead changes, finding the correct takeoff for a fence, or calculating a landing just right, but then I catch myself anticipating the next mistake because I have this mentality that says, "Why would I possibly do two things correct in a row? If I just did something right, something wrong is surely going to happen any minute." I realize that it's a horrible way to think, but I can't control the thoughts in my head while I'm riding.

I did mention before that I had not one, but several trainers who were way too harsh on me. I didn't know that then; I thought I was learning from them as long as the insults were less and less harsh and frequent. I have finally learned that what I am doing right is so much more important than what I am doing wrong.

Nevertheless, I still have those thoughts in my head: "There's no way you'll make that jump," or "You're not good enough to get the changes in that combination to make it right," or "Are you even listening to what I'm saying or do you choose to do everything the wrong way?" I understand now that these are not progressive teaching techniques, but that doesn't stop those negative voices in my head. The positive things my new trainer says is definitely a big help, but I need to get control of all of the negative stuff that is still there and sometimes takes over.

Clearly, Sasha had some challenges and had not always been surrounded by supportive, positive influences. *My* challenge was to retrain her brain by removing the old, destructive patterns and thoughts that were conditioned responses, and replacing them with words and imagery that would create optimistic internal language and lead to peak performance. The following are helpful to anyone, in any situation, who is paralyzed by the memories or the effects of past abuse of any kind.

- Disengaging the negative thoughts and patterns from your subconscious mind so you can move forward. (I use a technique called Release and Clear, which will be detailed in a moment.)
- Changing your perspective on the past by gathering new information. (I use reframing for this.)
- Creating an image of the desired performance. This image acts as a road map of the correct, optimal way of executing a move, a jump, or anything else. (I use the technique known as Theater of the Mind to accomplish this.)
- Instantly triggering a desired response by using an anchor. For example, I told Sasha that every time she sits in her saddle, she is relaxed and every time she holds the reins, she is alert, breathes rhythmically, and performs at her peak level.
- Providing a real-life example of someone who has reached the desired level of competence. (I use Modeling to create this.)
- Surrounding yourself with people, sights, and sounds that contribute to high-level performance. (In NLP, we call this the Circle of Excellence.)
- Developing a new language to be used for internal thinking and external speech, which will eventually create behavior that is consistent with the language.

Let's look at how one simple word can powerfully transform your self-talk . . .

Mary's Story

For some reason, negative thoughts always creep into my mind when I ride. There are a wide array of these negative thoughts that may include any combination of the following: My horse will probably cut that corner, I will miss that lead change, I will probably chip that fence with the long approach, I bet you I am going to chip at the brush box, and there is no way that I can hold the countercanter that long. I don't know why I do this to myself, but I just can't seem to get these thoughts out of my mind.

After hypnotizing Mary and introducing her to the CANCEL technique . . .

I realize now what I was doing wrong. I was setting myself up to make mistakes because I was thinking a negative thought. Laura hypnotized me to say the word cancel and replace the negative thought with a positive one. Now, when a negative thought enters my mind, it is so easy to just cancel out that thought. Eliminating negative thinking from my thought processes has changed my riding. The key to riding successfully is to eliminate all of this negative programming. Since I fill my mind with positive thoughts, I get positive results. It was so easy to change the way I was thinking. She also used several NLP techniques with the hypnosis and put the suggestion in my subconscious mind that every time I see the color red I think positive thoughts about my riding ability. As an added measure and as a reminder to be positive, I have safety-pinned a swatch of red onto the top of my show coat above my wrist. It really works. It's amazing how we can retrain the mind to be able to control our own thoughts and eliminate the thoughts that might have been created or put there by a past negative trainer. Plus I have always been one of those people who really believed in Murphy's Law, always thinking about the negative so I am prepared for it. But now I find that I need to concentrate on the outcome of what I really want to be able to practice and visualize the positive to happen. Laura taught me so much about being the person that I think I am. I am what I think. Therefore, I am choosing to be positive.

Self-Hypnosis to Transform Your Self-Talk: Instant Alpha Conditioning

Instructions:

1. Use the word you selected to replace the alpha conditioning technique introduced in Chapter 4. Read the following script and let alpha occur.

2. Then proceed to the script for Release and Clear and/or Positive Self-Talk.

From this moment on, each and every time I desire to attain the deep state of total relaxation, I am instantly and fully relaxed, as I am now drifting into the alpha state of consciousness. The moment I think my chosen word _____, alpha occurs. This word has an effect only when I use it and only under the proper circumstances. Each and every time I do use it I am fully prepared to receive positive, beneficial, and constructive suggestions, impressing each one deeper into the storage and memory facility of my brain.

From this moment on, _____ triggers deep relaxation of my mind and body. I feel alpha occur. I feel wonderful. I feel comfortable. I am totally receptive and responsive to my own creative ideas and suggestions. I am bathed in a glow of quietness, peace, and serenity. My chosen word works only when I deliberately use it for deep relaxation to attain alpha consciousness. Its use in regular conversation has no effect on me whatsoever. From this moment on, each and every time I desire the deep state of total relaxation, I am instantly and fully relaxed upon saying _____. Because my subconscious must follow my command, each and every time I desire total relaxation, I am instantly and fully relaxed when I think my chosen word _____. I feel a deep sense of gratification as this word programming becomes a reality. Feeling wonderful, generous, alive, and eager to awaken . . .

Twenty minutes, wide awake.

Release and Clear

If negative thoughts, memories, or other images tend to creep into your mind and invade your thinking while you are riding, this simple technique will help release your mind from thinking about (or even obsessing over) those negatives so you can move on and use your brain for more productive things.

Instructions:

1. Read each night, before retiring, for 21 nights. If you miss a night, you must begin again. Read aloud, with feeling.

S	M	T	W	Th	F	Sat

2. Say the words "release and clear" every night thereafter.

So relaxed . . . so relaxed . . . slowly drifting into a most satisfying state of relaxation. Relaxation is good for me. I release every last ounce of useless tension . . . as I rest contentedly, to awaken when I must, refreshed and invigorated. I am alive with the feeling of freedom, of promise, of exhilarating positive expectation. My mind is clear . . . my body recharged . . . and my past deactivated . . . and left behind me.

As I relax . . . I release every unhappy experience of the past . . . and everything connected with those experiences. I find it easy to let them go. I am a part of life . . . as are we all . . . and we all move, live, and think, as we have a right to. Life goes on, and so do I . . . growing rich in experience . . . and in capacity to achieve. My positive experiences supply me with a directness to meet the challenges of my life. All I must do is use the amazing power of my subconscious mind. I am using that capacity now to disengage me from every negative . . . destructive . . . and harmful impression ever made upon me. They fade . . . fade . . . fade out of my life forever.

I am grateful and thankful for every experience of the past. I now forgive myself for every mistake I have ever made; and I forgive everyone else who may have in any way harmed me. I know that out of each experience . . . as I understand it . . . good must surely come to me. I forgive myself for every mistake because I know that each mistake is a stepping-stone to greater understanding . . . to greater opportunity . . . and to greater achievement. I grow stronger with each experience . . . and I am stronger than anything life can offer. I am preparing myself to meet its challenges directly . . . free of negative conditioning. I am more than any challenge . . . for I possess the power and the ability to channel any experience into a rich and rewarding way of life.

I now fully release the past . . . and all its effects upon me. I am free . . . free of the past . . . free to be me . . . entirely. I accept myself completely. I am a valuable and talented human being . . . I am always aware of my innate worth. There are things to be done by me . . . that are done better by me than by any other human being. Every word . . . every movement . . . every gesture of mine . . . preserves my unique stamp upon life. For as long as time has been . . . or ever shall be . . . there is no one who can exactly duplicate me. I am pleased . . . I accept myself . . . I love myself . . . I am grateful for my new level of understanding. My acceptance releases me from negative self-dislike . . . and so I am now free to change that which must be changed . . . to improve that which can be improved . . . to let go of that which is inhibiting or destructive. My self-acceptance now enables me to accept everyone else . . . I accept myself . . . I accept others as they are . . . I accept even those who are unacceptable . . . as unacceptable . . . and go on my way.

I bestow upon others my affection . . . true and unencumbered. In my imagination . . . I see them having all the good I desire for myself. What I desire for myself, I also desire for everyone else . . . I have fulfilled my nature. I have supplied myself with those priceless qualities and feelings . . . acceptance . . . love . . . and forgiveness . . . and so I now have them to give. I give them freely. I feel the warmth and excitement of building a new and rewarding life. A firm, quiet sense of self-love and self-determination dominates my every waking and sleeping hour. I am ready to release, and do so this night. CLEAR . . . CLEAR . . . CLEAR.

Twenty minutes, wide awake.

Once you've done the instant alpha and then Release and Clear if you needed it, proceed to self-hypnosis for positive self-talk.

Positive Self-Talk

When negative thoughts enter my mind about horseback riding, I mentally say the word "cancel" to myself. I replace any negative thought that I may have with a positive thought. Positive thoughts remain within the conscious portion of my mind much longer and much clearer than ever before. Without fail, without exception, without excuse, each and every time a negative thought or idea enters my mind, I mentally say the word "cancel" to myself. My personal life is in order, my private life is content, and my health is in perfect order. I see myself how I want to be. I am positive, happy, healthy, and glad to be alive.

I know that being positive, happy, healthy, and being glad to be alive is called being "in the zone." I am in the zone when I ride. I understand that being in the zone is when I feel that I am winning all of the time . . . it is an unstoppable, powerful confidence that means that I am the best that I can be. I am always absolutely doing and achieving what I set my mind to do. I am thankful that through the power of positive thinking I have the ability to create positive actions. My internal positive self-talk allows me to achieve whatever outcomes I want to work toward. I know that when I practice positive self-talk, my subconscious mind allows positive thoughts to flow through to the conscious mind.

Every day that I ride, I am physically stronger and fitter. I am more alert, more wide-awake, and more energetic. Every day that I go to the stables, I remain so deeply interested in whatever I am doing. When I ride, my mind is much less preoccupied with myself and I am much less conscious of myself. I focus on my task at hand. Every day that I ride my nerves are stronger and steadier. When I am on a horse, my mind is calm, clear, and composed. I think clearly . . . I concentrate easily . . . my memory is sharp . . . I see things in their true perspective and do not allow them to get out of proportion. Every day that I ride a horse, I am emotionally calm and tranquil. I feel a wonderful sense of personal well-being, personal safety, and security.

I am completely relaxed and tranquil. I have confidence in myself and in my ability to ride, perform, compete—whatever I ought to be able to do. I am optimistic, happy, and confident. I stick up for myself . . . I stand on my own feet . . . I hold my own ground. Things happen exactly as I wish for them to happen in and out of the riding arena. I remain cheerful and optimistic.

No matter what is going on in my life, I always remain positive and free from negative self-talk. I am confident in my riding abilities and "cancel" out any negative and harmful self-talk that I may have. I remain with a clear outlook for a wonderful and successful future in and out of the riding arena. Every time I see the color red, it reminds me that I will be positive and in the zone.

This entire suggestion is represented by the letter *H* of my sub-key word, RHYTHM. Anytime I think, say, or see the word RHYTHM, all suggestions keyed to this word are automatically activated, stimulated, and work for my benefit.

Twenty minutes, wide awake.

CHAPTER 6

GAINING CONCENTRATION

Your Focus: From Scattered to Optimal Concentration

Concentration upon a single idea has been the hallmark of success for countless people and organizations.

—Napoleon Hill,
Keys to Success: The 17 Principles
of Personal Achievement

The single idea you want to concentrate your attention on is something like: "achieving peak performance in my riding."

People with concentration challenges usually talk a lot about having difficulty "staying focused." They are easily distracted by:

- The other horses around them
- Golf carts going by
- The person on the loudspeaker reading announcements
- Who is watching (e.g., a spouse, a trainer, an ex-trainer)
- The presence of people who may be interested in buying their horses

Basically, their brains are occupied with everything but what they are supposed to be doing. All of this busyness occurs on the conscious level, and it's all so loud to them that we have to do a lot of work to get them to the point where their subconscious is able to block out all of the unimportant information that surrounds them.

What is Concentration?

Concentration is the effortless ability to stay focused, and in the present, on the tasks that you need master in order to achieve your peak performance. We all have this ability, but most of us have difficulty concentrating consistently and *when we know we need to.*

Excellent Concentration is Learned

Fortunately, if your concentration isn't great you can improve it dramatically with some practice. (And a bonus of increasing your concentration is that your memory will improve, as well.) Hypnosis will unblock whatever is preventing your subconscious from achieving maximum concentration. But just as with positive self-talk, relaxation, and releasing performance anxiety, the best results occur when the power of hypnosis is bolstered by exercises you can do on the conscious level.

Concentration Busters

It's not that difficult for most people to lose their concentration; it doesn't take much. Here are the most common causes for loss of focus when you're riding:

- Anxiety—Perhaps you're concerned about the quality of your competition or your horse's readiness.
- Lack of Confidence—When your confidence is low, too much mental energy is wasted on second-guessing your talents and abilities.
- Distractions—It could be outside noises from the crowd or even unrelated concerns from your personal life.
- Boredom—It can be easy to let your mind wander while you are engaged in an activity you've mastered.

What Happens When Your Concentration Is Lacking

When you aren't able to concentrate, your body tends to get stiff. You tend to hold the reins in a non-flexible way because you are so tense, and fixed hands make it difficult to gauge the horse's stride. Furthermore, your stomach and legs tighten. Once you are in this position, you horse feels your tension and usually reacts by getting nervous. Your horse knows when you're afraid. If you concentrate on being supple, you'll both be comfortable and able to perform.

Eliminating Potential Distractions Is Impossible

The most effective way to improve your concentration is *not* to seek to eliminate distractions, but to change your relationship to them. In other words, you alter the way you experience the things, people, sounds, and information around you. You choose to experience them as neutral, rather than as disruptive. You acknowledge that they exist, and then forget about them. When you do this, your brain is able to focus better because it is no longer drawn to sounds, sights, and feelings that you ordinarily experience as distracting.

Luckily, there is one technique, which can be used in myriad ways that can instantly help you with your concentration: attention, or rather, *attending* to something.

Things to Do:

I use one simple technique with my clients that anyone can do, wherever they are. You don't have to be riding for this exercise. All you need is one word . . . or maybe two or three . . . Here are some versions of the attention exercise, and of changing your relationship to things you may experience as distractions:

Handling the Noise Inside Your Head

- Attend to your thoughts during the day, and when you notice them wandering, say to yourself: "concentrate," "be present," "be here now," or your own mantra if you already have one.

The more attention you give to your thoughts, the more you'll realize that they wander around a great deal during the day. Just remember that each time they wander, you can retrieve them back to the present and the task at hand.

- Reward yourself. When you've completed a task without having to use your mantra dozens of times, reward yourself. Praise yourself for your accomplishment.

Handling the Noise Outside Your Head

- While you are riding or working or doing whatever you need to concentrate on during the day, practice allowing whatever noises or movements that occur around you do so without looking and reacting to them. Now, I'm not saying you should completely block out what is going on around you. This is about not being distracted by your surroundings, but being able to attend to anything you need to *despite* your surroundings. If you notice a sound or a movement, don't make a big deal out of noticing it; just move on to whatever you have to do.

- Reward yourself. When you've completed a task without attending to potential distractions in your surroundings, reward yourself. Praise yourself.

Advanced Concentration Exercise

- Sit in a comfortable chair in a quiet room where you won't be disturbed. Close your eyes and focus your attention on the space between your eyes. When you notice your attention moving away, notice where it went and bring it back.
- Repeat the exercise once again, this time with music with lyrics playing in the background. Is it harder to concentrate? Where does your mind go?
- If you can hold your attention on the space between your eyes for a full minute, you should have no problem concentrating on your event, regardless of outside distractions. If you think of a minute as a short amount of time, this exercise will give you a new perspective.

Focus isn't just a matter of inserting "concentration" into your subconscious. You have to work at broadening and deepening your awareness of what you are doing to subvert your focus, and do exercises to hone it, in addition to retraining your brain through hypnosis.

Jason's Story

Jason, an 11-year-old who had been riding for four years on several different horses and ponies, was brought to me by his mother. Jason's challenge was staying focused, concentrated, and balanced because he would get so excited and anxious about not doing well that he wasn't able to perform well. He also had difficulty with owners watching him and constantly filming him on their horses. All of this was a lot for an 11-year-old boy (or for anyone, I think), and it kept him from riding as well as he could.

When he entered my office he was nervous and wanted to know what I was going to "do to" him. I explained and he was excited. He was very easily hypnotized and enjoyed it. We used the word *focus,* and attached his focus on the task at hand to the word. We worked on "blanking out" the things and people he was experiencing as distracting.

When he returned for his next visit, he was so excited about how well it worked that he brought a list of things he wanted me to do for him. The second item on his list was that he wanted me to blank out his trainer like I had blanked out everyone else. And he said it was because the trainer always put him down and that hurt his feelings. I told him that it wouldn't be professional for me to do that, but I could block out the hurt and the pain connected to what was said, and that would make him perform better.

Another thing on his list was that he would get so excited when he did well that he would miss whatever followed his excitement, which was usually his next jump. I anchored in that he would be balanced after each go and ready for the next one.

Finally, we anchored in that every time he went to the practice ring or the show ring, no matter who was watching or filming, they were all anchors for him to concentrate easier and better. He didn't even notice anyone was there.

Jesse's Story

When I was young my father came to my very first horse show. I remember being so proud that my father took time out from his important schedule to watch me and my pony compete. But I also remember that my pony stopped at the first fence and I fell off. Now, whenever I ride in a show, I always feel like I'm either going to fall off at the first fence or at least chip at that fence. I just can't seem to get that thought out of my mind. It's so frustrating because I almost always screw up my first fence in some way. Just the thought of this makes me nervous for every horse show that I go to. I can't keep my mind on what I'm doing for long. It seems that I always want to look around and check out who's watching. This makes it so hard to concentrate. I hear every sound that happens around the ring. It's like my mind is wandering all the time.

Three weeks later . . .

Wow! I'm so proud of myself because I just finished my first horse show after listening to 21 sessions of "Concentration." I found that forgiving myself for the mistake that I made a long time ago has opened new doors for me. It has helped me step out of the box and stop letting my thoughts spin counterproductively. I've stopped letting my mind fuel the anxiety and interfere with my performance. By listening to the CD my body and mind have both changed. It's so easy to focus on what I'm doing. Now I'm so focused that it doesn't matter who is watching. I feel good about myself and notice that I'm very attentive to what my trainer is telling me to do. Every time I sit in my saddle I feel attentive to what I am doing and concentrate so easily.

The Concentration CD has worked so well that I decided to listen to another one of Laura's CDs: Peak Performance. This

CD changed my overall self-confidence and I feel better about myself than I have in a long time. The visualization sessions have been especially helpful and now my jumping rounds come off exactly as I planned. On course, I count my horse's strides and that automatically calms and relaxes me. When I'm in the show ring and I feel a bout of nerves coming on, I take a deep breath in, exhale, and count from ten to one slowly. What a difference there is when you have these techniques! And they're not just helpful for riding. I use them in other areas of my life, like when I have to give a presentation at work.

Leslie's Story

I love going to horse shows and competing. My goals for owning and showing horses all revolve around doing well and succeeding at competitions. I've been riding my entire life and I have a natural talent for it. I know I'm a good and competent rider; that's not my problem. My problem is that I get so nervous before I go into the show ring that it prevents me from having the perfect performance that I know I am capable of executing. I get so nervous that I totally freeze. I forget my courses, even though I've gone over them thousands of times in my head and even physically walked them!

I experience feelings very similar to symptoms of anxiety attacks. I know that the horse can feel my anxiety and nervousness, and most horses totally feed off of the rider's energy anyway, so this problem creates devastating consequences for both me and the horse I'm riding. I've been very fortunate to have horses that know the courses better than I do, and most of the time I have the ability to ignore my nervousness and just perform the way the horse was taught, but I'm not always that lucky. If I'm on a horse that isn't as finished or polished as some of the show veterans I have ridden, it's disastrous! It's very unprofessional for my horse and me to be unprepared and basically unglued in the show ring. It's nearly impossible for me to plan to make a profession out of riding and showing horses if I can't get control of my nervousness and my overall performances.

My issues have snowballed from a few simple show jitters into a condition that hinders everything about my performance. I fall apart in the show ring because I don't have control over what occurs in my head while I'm riding. And I honestly believe this is a psychological problem because I ride perfectly at home, where I'm comfortable, relaxed, and confident. But then, when I enter the show ring, I feel like everyone is watching me and judging me and I panic.

When I ride my mind isn't 100 percent concentrating on what I'm doing. Sometimes I don't even remember how it starts. It's like I'm distracted by something early on, but I still manage to ride. Before I know it, my performance has all kinds of flaws and is set up for a bunch of other flaws that it's too late to prevent.

The Problem

Leslie's language clearly indicates that her level of anxiety leads to a near-complete inability to concentrate while she is in the ring.

The Solution

■ As in the previous chapter, in Sasha's story of trainers who were harsh and abusive, Leslie's first mission is to eliminate the impact of the past by using the Release and Clear technique. Once Leslie's mind is no longer obsessing over negative thoughts and experiences from her past, she will be able to see possibilities and opportunities.

■ Difficulties with concentration are often triggered by a specific place, such as the show ring. Leslie and I reframed her experience of the ring; we shifted it from anxiety-producing and threatening to the feeling she gets when she is someplace safe and able to concentrate (her home). In other words, we made the show ring feel like home to Leslie.

■ To further alleviate Leslie's anxiety and improve her ability to concentrate, I used an anchor to trigger Leslie to slow down and breathe.

■ I also used an anchor to connect the activity of riding the horse to feeling good and relaxed every time.

■ I used Theater of the Mind to create a movie about Leslie's new, desired behavior and performance. Her mind will get accustomed to the perfect performance, it will be unable to distinguish it from reality, and it will then work to produce the performance.

The Result

After four visits over two months, I showed for the first time. I felt a complete difference in my ability to concentrate. I noticed that it was like I was on autopilot just doing what I was supposed to do. When I was in the show ring,

I was focused and didn't hear all of the chatter that had been yelling in my head for so long.

WHAT TO DO NOW:

If you need to use Release and Clear to stop focusing on a negative experience from the past, do so after Instant Alpha Conditioning and before the Gaining Concentration script. If you don't need to Release and Clear, simply proceed to Instant Alpha and then to Gaining Concentration.

Instant Alpha Conditioning

Instructions:

1. Use the word you selected to replace the alpha conditioning technique introduced in Chapter 4. Read the following script and let alpha occur.
2. Then proceed to the script for Gaining Concentration.

From this moment on, each and every time I desire to attain the deep state of total relaxation, I am instantly and fully relaxed, as I am now drifting into the alpha state of consciousness. The moment I think my chosen word _____, alpha occurs. This word has an effect only when I use it and only under the proper circumstances. Each and every time I do use it I am fully prepared to receive positive, beneficial, and constructive suggestions, impressing each one deeper into the storage and memory facility of my brain.

From this moment on, _____ triggers deep relaxation of my mind and body. I feel alpha occur. I feel wonderful. I feel comfortable. I am totally receptive and responsive to my own creative ideas and suggestions. I am bathed in a glow of quietness, peace, and serenity. My chosen word works only when I deliberately use it for deep relaxation to attain alpha consciousness. Its use in regular conversation has no effect on me whatsoever. From this moment on, each and every time I desire the deep state of total relaxation, I am instantly and fully relaxed upon saying _____. Because my subconscious must follow my command, each and every time I desire total relaxation, I am instantly and fully relaxed when I think my chosen word _____. I feel a deep sense of gratification as this word programming becomes a reality. Feeling wonderful, generous, alive, and eager to awaken . . .

Twenty minutes, wide awake.

By regularly using the following hypnosis script, you will be teaching your brain to block out all of the outside "noises" that prevent you from attending to the appropriate information. Retrain the brain to pay attention to your tasks at hand.

Gaining Concentration for the Equestrian

I am totally focused and attentive in my riding lessons and in the show ring. When I am riding a horse, just as a magnifying glass concentrates energy into a particular point of light, my mind excludes everything except the chosen task at hand. I am thankful for my ability to pay close attention to what my instructor is teaching . . . it is easy for me to concentrate during the classes that I compete in at horse shows. I am thankful for my ability to focus my faculties on a single purpose . . . I am thankful that I can concentrate on riding to achieve my peak performance.

I concentrate deeply and my ability to reason is alert. I know that I am a master of the art of concentration. I concentrate without effort. It is easy for me to focus and to keep my attention on my lesson or on the class that I compete in. I exclude all else from my mind, while still being certain that my well-being is foremost important.

I feel focused and attentive when I sit in my saddle. I ride with complete balance and I handle everything that my horse does with confidence and self-assurance. It is so easy for me to concentrate . . . I easily learn new skills and conquer new challenges. Concentration opens doors to new areas for me . . . I am pleased that as I gain concentration, my capacity for learning and for development expands. I am attentive to details in all areas of my riding experience. My ability to find a solution to a new challenge is rewarded with firmness of mind and clarity of purpose. I persevere until I am satisfied with the outcome of my specific endeavor.

My ability to concentrate is strengthened each time I mount my horse and sit in the saddle. Relaxation automatically increases my ability to concentrate. Concentration intensifies my mind and increases my awareness of my surroundings. I know that I desire to learn more . . . I solve whatever problems are before me. I become more relaxed and my concentration increases as I flow with my horse's movement.

My ability to concentrate reinforces all that I learn in my lessons. I am so thankful that my ability to concentrate expands my mind. My mind automatically executes what I successfully accomplish in my lessons. My mind is open and eager to use all of the knowledge that it gains.

I persevere with determination in my desire to concentrate thoroughly on my riding. I succeed admirably and I am pleased with my efforts. I am pleased with my ability to be attentive to details. My ability to find solutions to challenges is increased as I pay attention with firmness of mind and clarity of purpose. I persevere until I am satisfied with the outcome of my encountered endeavors. The focus of my attention is strengthened each time I use my ability to concentrate, each time I get on my horse, and each time I sit in the saddle.

The more I ride, the more I master the art of concentration. Anytime I need assistance concentrating, I take a deep breath, exhale, and say the word "focus" quietly to myself. The word "focus" is a conditioned response key to my subconscious mind. When I say this word, I recapture my ability to concentrate while on my horse.

This entire suggestion is represented by the letter *Y* of my sub-key word, RHYTHM. Anytime I think, say, or see the word RHYTHM, all suggestions keyed to this word are automatically activated, stimulated, and work for my benefit.

Twenty minutes, wide awake.

CHAPTER 7

RELEASE OF PERFORMANCE ANXIETY
Your Emotional State: From Anxiety to the Zone

When you first learned how to ride a bicycle, you probably had a good dose of performance anxiety. There you were, with your mother watching and your father holding the seat and the handlebars, walking alongside you. You knew that your father was going to let go soon and you'd be riding *all by yourself.* If you were like most people, you were thinking of everything you had to do: balance, peddle, steer, sit up straight. Oh, and breathe and keep your eyes open.

That's an awful lot to think about, especially when your entire family is watching you. Your heart pounds, you think and think and think about all of the physical movements you have to keep track of, and you are so nervous and so hyper-aware that you actually recall having to send a signal from your brain to your feet to start peddling.

That's performance anxiety.

Now, fast forward one year, and picture yourself whizzing around the neighborhood, doing the slalom around the trees, hopping over curbs, and popping wheelies. You're in the zone. The only thing you're thinking about is beating your own record for speeding down the street. Your feet pedal as fast as they can, but know when to stop for an upcoming jump. Your arms put the handlebars up exactly at the right time, and you effortlessly lift your entire body—and your bike—a foot in the air to hop a large curb. You aren't conscious of any of this, yet it all happens.

That's "the zone." Peak performance, flow, the zone, your best performance . . . they all mean the same thing. You have no awareness of time or space, your focus is razor-sharp, your movements are fluid and spontaneous. And you're happy.

Hypnosis is a very important part of releasing performance anxiety because it turns the anxiety switch from "on" to "off." But hypnosis doesn't solve the problem completely. There is a lot of work you should do with your conscious self to help you relieve some of the physical and mental tension you experience about your upcoming performances. Here are some tips:

■ Be prepared.

No amount of hypnosis is going to help you if you aren't prepared to do your best. This includes practicing under conditions that are similar to what you'll experience during your upcoming performance. Eat right, sleep well, exercise, and do some deep breathing or meditating. Just as athletes regularly train their bodies to execute precise skills or maintain a certain pace, they need to regularly train their minds to think precise thoughts and focus on specific things.

■ Don't expect perfection.

Athletes train their physical skills for years, trying to achieve the perfect performance. I think I've seen perfect performances, but I sure wouldn't want to strive for perfection. As I've discussed previously, perfection assumes that there is always another level, and another level, and another level that you can reach. Just the notion of it is mentally exhausting and

debilitating to many people because they presumably will *always* strive
for it and *never* reach it.

When preparing for a horse show, you give yourself hundreds, maybe even
thousands, of suggestions. If your thoughts during this time are confident
and positive, your mind and body respond well, and you can enjoy great
performances. If your thoughts are concerned with pressuring yourself to
execute the perfect performance, the stress of that unreasonable expectation
will prevent you from enjoying yourself and hamper your performance.

■ Imagine peak performance.

Imagine yourself giving the optimal performance. Create a complete,
rich sensory experience. Imagine what you look like, what your horse
looks like, how you feel on your horse, what you smell, what you hear.
The more detailed your image is, the better. Note that imagining peak
performance and expecting perfection are *not* the same thing. And of
course, remember that your brain doesn't know the difference between
your memory of something real and something imagined. Imagining
doesn't have the pressure and emotion attached to it that *expectation* has.
Expectation can lead to disappointment; imagination cannot.

■ Control your environment.

You can't control everything, but you can control who you spend time
with and how you react to them. If there is someone in your life who

"pushes all of your buttons," either don't spend time with that person, or change the way you react to him and his behavior. (The latter is possible, but takes time. The former is a quicker, easier fix, but also can be viewed as cosmetic since it doesn't actually get to the core of the problem.)

■ Empower yourself with self-talk.

Assume success, imagine success, and you'll get it, providing you have done what you need to do to prepare for it.

■ Relax.

It's difficult when your attempts at relaxation are solely on a conscious level. Luckily, the exercises in Chapter 4 will help you alleviate some of the physical and emotional stress you feel when you're full of anxiety. And the Basic Relaxation script uses the subconscious to create relaxation that is deeper and more immediate than you'll be able to achieve on the conscious level.

■ Make your mistakes work for you.

In NLP we say *mistakes are just feedback*. Think about it. A mistake simply tells you that there is something you need to do differently. You might not immediately know what you need to do differently, but you can start experimenting as soon as you have received feedback: an outcome that you didn't want. Once you've recognized that you're making a mistake, you must make a commitment to not reproducing that mistake: a commitment to turn it around. What's crucial here is the desire to change. If you have no desire to change, you simply will not be able to. Therefore, ask yourself the question: "Do I really want to change behavior X?" If the answer is yes, make a conscious commitment to make your mistakes work *for* you, not against you. We'll be delving more into mistakes in Chapter 9, but for now, think about changing your relationship to them (just as you are working on changing your relationship to the things in your surroundings that you might call "distractions") and seeing them as useful information.

■ Be patient.

It has taken months or even years for you to develop the pattern mistakes that you are currently making. Once you have made a commitment to change your mistakes around to work for you, stick with that commitment. Don't give up. Everyone is different. Some riders may be able to fix their mistakes and turn them around by doing at-home sessions and exercises once a week. Other riders may need to listen to a self-hypnosis CD for 20 sessions a month. Meanwhile, other riders may need to enlist the assistance of a live hypnotist to help them overcome their fears, negative self-talk, or other self-inflicted ailments.

Things to Do:

Here are some exercises you can do to help alleviate your performance anxiety:

■ Be aware of your thoughts

Observe your thoughts as they run through your head. Don't try to stop or edit them—just let them go. Make a mental note of how many times, and to what degree, you worry, dwell on negatives, criticize yourself, think of something anxiety-provoking, or think of yourself as inadequate or a failure. Awareness is the first step toward developing positive thinking.

A great way to demonstrate to yourself just how absurd some of your thoughts are is to put them on paper. Write down negative thoughts as soon as they occur. You'll probably get a good laugh at some of the stuff that comes into your head, but once the amusement ends, you've got to get down to the business of making a change in your thought process.

■ Stop negative thoughts

Remember that your thoughts create your reality. Negative self-talk is destructive to your growth as a rider and a competitor. This seemingly simple exercise consists of four steps: (1) become aware of the negative self-talk; (2) stop the negative talk as soon as it occurs; (3) replace the negative talk with positive talk; and (4) repeat and practice this exercise as often as negative thoughts enter your mind.

Utilize the power of positive speech to erase negative thoughts from your vocabulary. At first, it won't be easy to erase them. Not only is your mind not used to having its thoughts interrupted, but your mind will also automatically fight the acceptance of the positive thought, merely because it is different; it's not what your mind is accustomed to. The only way to change this is through persistence. Make negative-thought stopping part of your daily routine.

■ Cultivate positive thinking

I'm referring to more than replacing your negative thoughts with positive ones, here. Cultivating positive thinking means creating a habit of optimism through affirmations and changing the way you use language on a day-to-day basis. It means striving to see the good in people rather than instantly recognizing the bad and focusing on it. It means creating positive habits, such as saying "please" and "thank you" and being compassionate and kind to the woman who checks out your groceries or waits on you at lunch, or the gentleman who picks up your garbage.

■ Practice positive visualization

This exercise should be done in a safe place that is devoid of major interruptions. You can practice positive visualization when you're sitting on your horse off to the side of the schooling arena, out of the flow of horse traffic. You can also practice positive visualization when you're lying in bed at night before you go to sleep or as soon as you awake in the morning.

There are several different strategies for positive visualization. I particularly like to have my clients visualize themselves in their mind, actually performing the task at hand. For example, lie in your bed in the morning and visualize yourself riding your horse successfully to each fence, and approaching each fence in a balanced and relaxed manner with an accurate spot at each fence every time. This type of visualization is entirely from your perspective: how you feel, what you see, what you are thinking, and what ultimately happens.

The flip side of visualizing how you feel is to picture yourself as a third party. Watch a movie of yourself riding. This is Theater of the Mind. For example, find a quiet place and visualize yourself riding a jumper course, executing all the proper turns with precision and pace. You're a spectator here, and you can use your imagination to create anything. What do you look like? What is around you? Pan around with your mental camera. What does your horse look like? Zoom in for a close-up on your horse's face. Then on your face. What would you have to be thinking and feeling in order to look like your close-up? Create those thoughts and feelings the next time you ride.

■ Model a rider whom you admire

The rider may be someone who is famous or may be a friend of yours whose riding skills you would like to emulate. Again, find a quiet place, perhaps in the spectator's seating at a local show, and visualize your face and body on that rider as she competes. Your intention is to observe another as if she were you. This particular technique is more advanced and takes more practice than the previous two. I suggest that you practice them first before moving on to this technique.

You will find that visualization is a comforting and peaceful experience. It has a calming affect upon you both mentally and physically. Your heart rate slows down and you feel a renewed sense of confidence.

■ Do simple breathing exercises

For immediate relief when you find yourself in a circumstance that makes you nervous or anxious, focus on your breathing. Take slow, deep breaths. When we are nervous, our breathing is immediately affected. It either becomes very quick and shallow, or comes to a virtual stop. By concentrating on taking slow, deep, methodical breaths, you: (1) take your mind off of the immediate situation that is making your nervous; (2) bring necessary oxygen to your organs and muscles, which will help you physically relax; and (3) slow your heart rate down so that it is no longer racing. You can practice this exercise anywhere and anytime. It's easy, inconspicuous, and fast-acting.

■ Use anchoring

As you know by now, anchors are commonly used in self-hypnosis and hypnosis to reinforce positive self-talk. Examples of anchors that you should be familiar with by now are the holding of the reins and the sensation of sitting in the saddle.

You can create your own anchors for use in the customized self-hypnosis scripts you'll be writing later. You can even start using them today, before you go to sleep. For example, if you show Western, maybe you'll choose touching the horn on your saddle as your anchor. Then, while you're lying on your bed, relaxing and breathing deeply this evening, simply say to yourself: "The moment I touch the horn on my saddle, I feel instantly calm and relaxed. . . . The moment I touch the horn on my saddle, I feel instantly calm and relaxed. . . . The moment I touch the horn on my saddle, I feel instantly calm and relaxed."

If you are a dressage rider, maybe your anchor will be the touching of your hat or the saluting of the judge. You may even choose a color as an anchor. Whatever you choose as your anchor, make sure that it is simple to use and uncomplicated to access.

- Forgive yourself

If and when you make a mistake, even after utilizing techniques to eliminate your mistakes, you must learn how to forgive yourself. You are human and humans make mistakes. You are not infallible; you're not perfect. The best athletes in the world and the most accomplished riders make mistakes. Remember that making mistakes is essential to your ability to make progress. Rather than counting your mistakes, learn from them and be thankful for the opportunity to learn. Remember, they're only feedback.

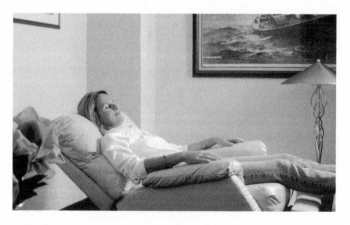

Renee relaxes completely and allows herself to access alpha.

- Use affirmations

Create first-person affirmations for yourself and read them to yourself, both silently and out loud, in the privacy of your own home or office.

Depending on your personal needs, you may want to read them once or twice a day, just a couple of days before a riding event, or all day long during the times when you are competing. The more often you read them, the more intense the affirmations will become. Read them like you mean it. Do not just mindlessly read the words. Focus on each sentence as you read it, and don't let yourself be distracted by outside noises or events.

Create affirmations that are personal to you and your specific situation or circumstance. Make sure to eliminate any negative talk and to clearly state the outcome you want as if it has already occurred—not that it will (you hope . . . you wish . . . you pray) occur. Write your affirmations neatly on large pieces of paper so that the words are easy to see and repeat. You can even laminate them to ensure that they are preserved and protected from the wear and tear of everyday use. Place a copy of your laminated affirmations in your horse-show bag or barn trunk to ensure that it is always there for inspiration. Place a laminated one in your shower.

■ List your mistakes

If you are a visual learner, I suggest that you write down a list of your goals. Your list should include a description of your mistake, a personal statement by you that you want to stop making this specific mistake, and then a statement on how you will accomplish your goal of turning this negative mistake into a positive experience.

■ Confide in a friend

It's unhealthy to keep negative thoughts and fears inside. Confiding in a friend is a healthy way to vent, as long as you choose your listener carefully.

■ Get expert help

Enlist the help of experts to assist you in making your mistakes work for you. Find a skilled hypnotherapist to visit. Make sure to check out her credentials. You can tell if the person is a skilled professional. Look for the initials "C. Ht." (certified hypnotist) after the name. Ask the professional where she studied and whom she studied under. Feel free ask for references. If the person is a true professional, she should be more than willing to give you such information to confirm her legitimacy.

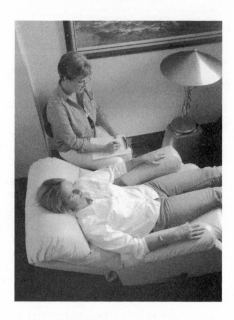

Caitlin's Story

I often think that I am not good enough to be riding at the
show barn that my trainer owns. It seems like all of his other
students are so tall, poised, and polished. I swear that everyone
else looks so perfect, and that I just don't fit in. I am scared to
go to a horse show because I feel like I would never live up to
a judge's standards. Whenever a show is scheduled, I always
tell my trainer that I have a scheduling conflict, even if I don't.
There is just no way I will be able to win a ribbon against all
that fierce competition out there. Everyone else in the show
ring just looks so much better than me. I decided that I need
to improve my personal thoughts about myself. To learn how
to like myself. Since I've always been put down by my parents
and my sister and brothers, it's really hard for me to do anything right. It seems that growing up the harder I tried to be
perfect, the more I was put down. This anxiety has affected
every aspect of my life. Realizing my lack of self-confidence
and lack of ability to perform in front of others, I decided to
get help.

After three sessions with Laura and two weeks of listening to the Release of Performance Anxiety CD . . .

I'm finally moving forward and have ridden in several shows. I have discovered that I'm a wonderful person with great talents. And I have a lot to share with other people. There's no reason why I can't ride just as well, if not better than everyone else. During my sessions with Laura, I learned about the difference between perfectionism and being perfect. I learned that by constantly driving myself to perfectionism, I was practically guaranteeing that everything I was doing wasn't going to be good enough. Once I came to the realization that at any given moment I am perfect in that moment and that everything else I do is in preparation to being perfect within the next moment, I started to feel so much lighter—like the weight of all of my anxiety was being lifted. Laura did several techniques to reduce the anxiety levels that I have attached to showing. And she also helped me see myself more objectively so I can recognize my abilities and talents. I learned to trust the natural-born talent and let it flow through me and just go into that wonderful zone where I'm on autopilot.

Instant Alpha Conditioning

Instructions:

1. Use the word you selected to replace the alpha conditioning technique introduced in Chapter 4. Read the following script and let alpha occur.
2. Then proceed to the script for Release of Performance Anxiety.

From this moment on, each and every time I desire to attain the deep state of total relaxation, I am instantly and fully relaxed, as I am now drifting into the alpha state of consciousness. The moment I think my chosen word _____, alpha occurs. This word has an effect only when I use it and only under the proper circumstances. Each and every time I do use it I am fully prepared to receive positive, beneficial, and constructive suggestions, impressing each one deeper into the storage and memory facility of my brain.

From this moment on, _____ triggers deep relaxation of my mind and body. I feel alpha occur. I feel wonderful. I feel comfortable. I am totally receptive and responsive to my own creative ideas and suggestions. I am bathed in a glow of quietness, peace, and serenity. My chosen word works only when I deliberately use it for deep relaxation to attain alpha consciousness. Its use in regular conversation has no effect on me whatsoever. From this moment on, each and every time I desire the deep state of total relaxation, I am instantly and fully relaxed upon saying _____. Because my subconscious must follow my command, each and every time I desire total relaxation, I am instantly and fully relaxed when I think my chosen word _____. I feel a deep sense of gratification as this word programming becomes a reality. Feeling wonderful, generous, alive, and eager to awaken . . .

Twenty minutes, wide awake.

Release of Performance Anxiety

I enjoy riding in competitions . . . I enjoy performing in front of others. I am self-reliant and comfortable being a winner when I perform. I release all performance anxiety I have ever experienced in the past . . . I release everything negative connected with those experiences. I am free from any fears of performance anxiety . . . free to be me. I accept myself completely . . . I love myself.

When I picture myself before a group of spectators, I take in a deep breath and then exhale completely. This makes me relaxed and centered inside. I smile and feel at ease as I imagine myself performing in front of others. I am confident in my ability to be calm. When, in reality, I am before a group of spectators, I take a deep breath and then exhale completely. This always makes me feel relaxed and centered on the inside. I smile at the prospect of having the opportunity to perform before others.

I am thankful for the opportunity to ride in a show to test myself against other competitors. I enjoy riding in performances in order to test my own talents and abilities. When I ride, my mind is occupied only with the task at hand. I know that I ride well . . . I know that I am skilled . . . I know that I am talented. I am well prepared to meet my goals. I give each class that I compete in my full attention. It is easy for me to focus on every corner and on every stride. I execute every move with style and precision.

I am a winner . . . I enjoy riding horses . . . I enjoy competing to test my abilities . . . My attitude is positive and full of fun . . . I focus my attention on the horse that I am riding . . . I keep my concentration as long as I want to . . . I am decisive and make correct decisions easily . . . I am consistent because I am focused . . . my body and mind are in perfect harmony . . . I give each stride my full intention and attention. I am proud of myself . . . I behave like a winner . . . I have all the traits of a winner . . . I know that I deserve to ride well . . . I know that I deserve to win the class. I am a true competitor and sportsperson.

If a performance doesn't come off as planned, I deal with any mistakes in a calm and effective manner. I take any mistakes that may occur in stride. I do not accept negative thoughts or feelings. I handle all situations easily and effectively, which separates me from the other riders. I am thankful that I meet any challenge before me with ease. I am ready for any challenge. I ride with confidence and poise.

I am a winner. Success moves throughout my entire body and makes me feel wonderful. I give each riding performance 100 percent of my attention. Each successful challenge that I conquer is imprinted on my subconscious mind as a blueprint that is recalled at any moment in time. My mind applies this blueprint to my mind-body connection so that my muscle memory is always there for me to achieve peak performance.

I enjoy riding, performing, and competing in front of others because I enjoy sharing my skills and talents with other people. I enjoy being successful . . . I feel like a winner through and through. I am secure and confident. Positive radiance shines from me.

Every time I want to relax before I compete, I hold my horse's reins and repeat the word "relax" silently to myself. "Relax" . . . "relax." I take a deep breath in and then exhale . . . "relax." The energy of being a winner surges throughout my entire body. I feel at ease and in total control. I am confident and calm with my competition skills. This inner warmth that I feel grants me happiness and success in the competition ring.

This special cue of holding my reins, breathing, and saying the word "relax" to myself always works for me in this way. Whenever I need to relax and release any performance anxiety, I squeeze my reins, breathe, and say the word "relax" silently to myself. My body feels wonderful, powerful, focused and in control.

This entire suggestion is represented by the letter *T* of my sub-key word, RHYTHM. Anytime I think, say, or see the word RHYTHM, all suggestions keyed to this word are automatically activated, stimulated, and work for my benefit.

Twenty minutes, wide awake.

CHAPTER 8

FEARLESS SHOWING AND JUMPING
Your Mental State: From Fearful to Fearless

Fear makes the wolf bigger than he is.
—German proverb

- What is your biggest fear when riding or about your riding?
- Are there people around you who feed your fears?
- How do you feel when you are around them?
- How many times a day do you feel fearful?
- Is there a payoff to feeling fearful?
- Is there a cost to feeling fearful?
- Does fear affect your decision-making?
- What are you attached to (e.g., are you fearful of losing)?
- Where does your fear show up?

Regardless of your particular fear profile, your fears hold you back from achieving peak performance and from feeling happiness, self-worth, and inner peace. In this chapter, I'll examine what fear is and how it affects you mentally and physically, and I'll discuss what you can do—today—to rid yourself of the fears that are keeping you from becoming the rider you can be.

What is Fear?

Fear is a painful emotion triggered by the apprehension of (real or imagined) danger, terror, displeasure. I say real or imagined because many of our fears are merely concoctions of our imagination. But as I have discussed so many times, your subconscious mind cannot distinguish between real images and imagined ones. It will produce the same fear response throughout the body for both. And then, as you probably know by now, what you fear is then likely to become your reality.

Some Fear Is Not Just Imagined—but Irrational!

As you probably know, the most common fear is of public speaking. It's more common than the fear of death (which, in case you were wondering, weighs in at number 7). This is a perfect example of how irrational fear can be. Let's say you are indeed afraid of public speaking. What exactly is it that you are afraid of? Is public speaking a life and death situation for you? For *anyone?* Are you even likely to be physically hurt in any way as a result of public speaking, even if you are terrible at it?

No.

Fear is your mind's way of making a potentially embarrassing or uncomfortable situation seem greater than it really is. Essentially, fear makes mountains out of molehills, and prevents us from enjoying our lives, our riding, and the calculated risks we take. You may have even heard FEAR defined as False Evidence Appearing Real.

How Does Fear Affect You Physically?

Once the mind gets the signal that there is something to fear (whether or not there is, in reality), it releases hormones throughout the body that trigger defensive chemical mechanisms. This is the "fight or flight" response we've all heard about and experienced.

- A message is sent to your hypothalamus, which regulates the stress response, to be on high alert.
- Your hypothalamus sends out signals preparing you for your response.
- Within nanoseconds, blood rushes to the center of your body, increasing your heart rate and your blood pressure, and then your muscles tense.

- Your hands and feet get cold and sweaty and you're ready to fight— or flee.
- Fear stimulates chemical releases in the brain that block thinking and concentration and immobilize you. Fear can make you completely freeze and be unable to perform. (And it's scary to be immobilized when you're on a horse about to jump over a five-foot fence.)
- If you are in the presence of something that could realistically cause you physical harm, you have anywhere from a few seconds to a few minutes to respond, and either flee or defend yourself.

Your body will go into the same full-blown fight-or-flight response when you are approaching a jump as it does when you are jumping out of a plane or off a cliff.

And then . . .

Burnout Can Occur

The fight-or-flight mechanism isn't meant to be triggered multiple times in a short period of time. As you may have noticed, when it *is* triggered, you usually experience the physical cues as stress because you do rationally know that your life is *not* in danger. But stress after stress eventually leads to exhaustion and burnout.

Conquering Fear

> **Fearless:** calmly resolute in facing real or
> imagined dangers or perils. Freedom from fear.

To overcome your fear, you must first identify where and when you
learned it. Is it rational? Irrational? Either way, it is real to you in your
mind, and sometimes once you acknowledge the origin as irrational, it
becomes easier to overcome.

Consider this . . .

Katy's first horse shied whenever he saw paper on the ground. For
some reason, it terrified him, which in turn terrified her. When she got
her second horse, Katy herself would get terrified when she saw paper on
the ground, which in turn terrified that second horse. Katy did the following to overcome her unique situation:

- She decided to face her fear. You have two choices with your fears:
  face them or be paralyzed by them. Katy spent some time being
  paralyzed, then decided to take action. She believed in the ability
  to change her fear and was resolute that it wasn't going to control
  her any longer. And that was half the battle.

■ She wrote her story. This is what I call a fear profile, and it's the history—the biography—of your fear. Frankly, once Katy saw her fear profile in writing, she immediately overcame it consciously, as her particular fear, though understandable, wasn't all that rational. This helped her reframe her situation and realize that while she had conditioned her second horse to shy when he saw paper on the ground, re-programming him was just as possible as re-programming herself.

Whether your fear is of a past experience recurring or of something new (e.g., fear of the unknown, fear of a new jump, a new ring, or a new way of entering a ring), that fear tends to be relived over and over again until it has snowballed to such a point that it is all-consuming.

You might think that I am going to help you eliminate your fear, but actually there is no such thing. Instead, we aim for mastery of the fear. As Mark Twain once said, "Courage is resistance to and mastery of fear— not the absence of fear." In order to master your fear, you must identify it and get to know it well.

Exercises to Help You Master Your Fears

■ Write your *fear profile*

Everyone should begin here and do this exercise at least once with each fear. Give your fear a name and write its biography. When did it come into your life? Why? Describe the day, if you recall, and/or the circumstance. As when you are doing a Theater of the Mind exercise, compose a story with rich sensory details. Often the mere creation and writing of the story deepens your understanding of your fear and helps you master it. Remember, you cannot master something if you don't know it well.

■ Instant change of state

The instant an unpleasant thought enters your mind, simply assure yourself that "the most powerful experience of this moment is the relaxation I am feeling." When you say this, you are diminishing the power of the fear and its effect on you. You are taken to a place of safety and serenity so that your body can use its precious resources on showing and jumping rather than on overreacting.

Face your fears slowly to desensitize yourself to their effects. And repeat your exposure to them over and over again until you realize that the dread in your head is much greater than the actual potential for harm.

Consider this: After Katy wrote her fear profile, her conscious mind was well aware of how irrational her fear was. But that didn't stop her subconscious mind from producing the fear response whenever she saw paper on the ground.

In order to desensitize herself (and her horse), she walked alongside her horse, 21 times, in the presence of paper on the ground. Then she mounted her horse and they walked, 21 more times, in the presence of paper. Once she was confident that she had mastered her fear, because her body chemistry was not producing a fear response, Katy's horse was not getting a cue of anxiety, tension, and apprehension. Katy's confidence and relaxation was felt by her horse, and they both mastered their fear.

■ Breathwork

The in-breath followed by the out-breath represents tension and release. And when the breath is blocked, the body and mind are blocked and in a state of substandard performance. There must be freely flowing breath in order for there to be peak performance. When you disconnect from your breath, you prevent flow; you get lost on your way to the zone.

■ Blowing Your Fears Away

Find a quiet place and breathe deeply, slowly, and completely. Visualize the thing, event, or person that is at the center of your biggest fear. See everything about the moment you fear most, then add more sensory details. Feel that moment of your biggest fear. Smell it. Hear it.

Then . . .

Shrink it.

Continue to shrink the picture in your mind until it is so small that when you hold it in the palm of your hand you can barely see, feel, smell, or hear it.

Then . . .

Blow on it once, and send it off into oblivion, never to return.

Cheryl's Story

I have ridden a lot of difficult horses. Even if they were bucking, bolting, and spooking it didn't scare me. Jumping does. Jumping has always made me nervous. I began jumping in college (25 years ago) with a trainer who went straight from cross rails to three-foot fences, and I was SO terrified, my heart would begin to pound when I got in the car to go to the stables. I somehow managed to conceal this fear, but it has underscored and undermined my jumping since then. I never became comfortable enough with it to feel secure, although I've hunted a fair amount, and different trainers have had me jump a number of green horses over the years. I'm a good quiet rider with a lot of experience. Specifically, all of my problems with jumping hinge on one thing: I have to fight myself at every jump not to move ahead of the horse. When I feel confident, I win the fight. When I'm nervous, I don't. I know better than to move ahead; it's not a matter of knowing or of inexperience. I've been told I have lovely form over fences—jumping feels wonderful when I can manage to sit still and wait. I really want to show. It's something that I believe is part of the reason to ride. I want to compete and enjoy it. It would give me something to focus on that I'd feel good about—I'd feel proud of myself for overcoming a fear and moving on.

Three months later . . .

It is so amazing that after working with Laura I'm able to perform consistently and I'm making progress every time I ride. It's good for me because I'm having positive thoughts about my riding. Every time I sit in my saddle I feel a wonderful feeling flow through me that I'm comfortable and able to do what I want. It's like I'm sitting and waiting for every jump with my horse. Using a few of my anchor words gives me the feeling of being bold and confident. When I am jumping now I'm so fluid, when anything doesn't come off as expected, I repeat my key trigger word: Pace. This gets me right back into the motion of moving with balance and harmony. And then I focus on the next fence. It's so cool how she hypnotized me to relax and breathe any time I count.

So when I'm counting strides I feel good and focused with the mere thought of numbers. My showing is really coming along, and now I want to really get myself ready to move into a new division. I have also noticed a new feeling of happiness and I have positive thoughts more often. I accept myself and see the positive actions and feeling overflowing into my business life. I really like how I feel.

Overcoming a Past, Serious Injury

A new client who had fallen and been injured was referred to me. After recovering from his injury, he wanted to go back to riding. Every time he got on his horse, his thoughts of falling off were stronger than anything he was doing. By allowing this fear to take over, he continued to fall off day after day.

He had an intense desire to ride and adored his horses. It was very important to him to ride and he received so much pleasure from it. He wanted to be able to get back to the basics and get on his horse and feel good and enjoy himself. He worked hard to be able to afford it, and he wanted to get back to feeling in sync with the horse. We worked on releasing and clearing his past experience, and then we worked on his self-confidence.

When you experience trauma, you tend to lose some of your self-worth and your confidence in your ability to do what you failed at before. This particular client didn't trust himself to get back in the saddle and ride again. Through hypnosis I did some NLP and anchoring so that every time he was in the saddle he felt self-confident, and he was careful and safe. When I emerged him from his hypnosis session, he was shocked at how good he felt. He said he felt better than he had in a long time.

He came back for his second visit and he felt great because he had enjoyed getting on his horse. He wasn't jumping yet, but he did feel like he accomplished a lot. He wanted to retrain his brain to being more confident about being in the saddle again. He wanted to accept his natural-born talent in riding, including jumping. He wanted the inner strength that can come from confidence. He wanted to feel happier about life and enjoy it more.

I hypnotized him again and created the way he wanted to be and ride: sitting in the saddle, proud of himself. We attached all kinds of direct suggestion to allow him to feel like he belongs in the ring. His saddle was his self-confidence zone, even when he was jumping.

By his third visit, he was jumping, confident, and relaxed in the saddle. He felt like his head was clear and he was more consistent than he had been in a long time. And he was loving every minute of it.

Self-Hypnosis for Fearless Showing and Jumping: Instant Alpha Conditioning

Instructions:

1. Use the word you selected to replace the alpha conditioning technique introduced in Chapter 4. Read the following script and let alpha occur.
2. Then proceed to the script for Fearless Showing and Jumping.

From this moment on, each and every time I desire to attain the deep state of total relaxation, I am instantly and fully relaxed, as I am now drifting into the alpha state of consciousness. The moment I think my chosen word _____, alpha occurs. This word has an effect only when I use it and only under the proper circumstances. Each and every time I do use it I am fully prepared to receive positive, beneficial, and constructive suggestions, impressing each one deeper into the storage and memory facility of my brain.

From this moment on, _____ triggers deep relaxation of my mind and body. I feel alpha occur. I feel wonderful. I feel comfortable. I am totally receptive and responsive to my own creative ideas and suggestions. I am bathed in a glow of quietness, peace, and serenity. My chosen word works only when I deliberately use it for deep relaxation to attain alpha consciousness. Its use in regular conversation has no effect on me whatsoever. From this moment on, each and every time I desire the deep state of total relaxation, I am instantly and fully relaxed upon saying _____. Because my subconscious must follow my command, each and every time I desire total relaxation, I am instantly and fully relaxed when I think my chosen word _____. I feel a deep sense of gratification as this word programming becomes a reality. Feeling wonderful, generous, alive, and eager to awaken . . .

Twenty minutes, wide awake.

Fearless Showing and Jumping

I am self-assured and confident in my ability to ride and compete. I use positive and empowering self-talk to achieve my goals. I am in control of my life. I no longer have fear-based emotions. I relax and release every fearful experience of the past and everything connected with those experiences. It is so easy to let go of my fears. My positive experiences supply me with the energy to meet all the challenges that I encounter when I ride. My subconscious mind has the amazing ability to disengage me from every negative and harmful impression ever made upon me.

I am grateful and thankful for every experience of the past. I forgive myself for every mistake I have ever made; and I forgive everyone else who may have in any way harmed me. I know that good comes out of each experience. I forgive myself for greater opportunities and I look forward to greater achievements. I grow stronger with each and every experience . . . I am stronger than anything life can offer. I am prepared to meet any riding challenge that I encounter in a state of mind that is free from negative thoughts. I possess the power and the ability to channel any occurrence into a rich and rewarding experience.

I am open to new suggestions, which I accept and act upon. I am open to all the warmth, joy and fulfillment that showing has to offer. I feel glad to be alive and enthusiastic about my future. I am thankful that I have the opportunity to show and compete. I am calm and relaxed and a sense of peace permeates my body and mind. I fully release the past fears and all the effects that these fears have had upon me. I am free . . . free of the past fear of showing . . . free to be me entirely. I accept myself completely . . . I am a valuable and talented human being . . . I am always aware of my innate worth. There are things that I do that are done better by me than by any other human being. There is no one who can exactly duplicate me . . . I accept myself . . . I love myself. I am grateful for my new level of understanding.

I easily visualize myself riding in competitions. I love the powerful feeling that riding my horse brings to me. I enjoy the harmony and balance of my horse as I hear the sound of the hooves patting the ground. I thoroughly enjoy these feelings as I ride. I am confidant and poised when I compete.

In order to prepare to compete when I am at a horseshow, I go through my round quietly in my mind. My mind is serene as I take slow deep breaths and allow quiet to occupy my insides . . . I spend several minutes going over the round in my mind . . . I relax and breathe . . . relax and breathe . . . relax and breathe. Calm and trust is all that is right. If there are any unnecessary internal voices, I use counting so that my unconscious mind can assume control of my body and its reactions. One . . . relax, two . . . breathe . . . three, four, five . . . relax, six . . . breathe, seven, eight . . . relax and breathe . . . nine, ten. Counting calmly puts me into a state of relaxation. I feel composed and free of tension . . . my breathing is slow and even. When I count the strides between my fences I relax and breathe.

Showing my horse is such a pleasant experience. I become totally immersed in the experience of competing. The fluid and graceful tempo of my horse is the rhythm of my body and my horse working together. I physically anchor the calm and wonderful feeling of competition by touching my right thumb and forefinger together as if I am holding my reins in each hand. This is my trigger that anchors these pleasant feelings of calm and confidence as I compete. I am confident, calm and relaxed every time I hold my reins.

It is calming for me to picture in my mind a successful jump or a successful go. It is easy for me to prepare my mind by simply going through my routine mentally—I visualize my round and this makes me calm. I am completely certain about the ride I am about to have. When it is my turn to enter the ring to compete, I breathe deeply to relax my mind and body. I center my body on my horse and I become perfectly comfortable as I hold the reins in my hands, touching my anchor to calm and relax me.

I feel self-assured, light, supple, poised, composed, and confident at the prospect of a successful ride. I ride my horse with rhythm, tempo, balance, and harmony. As I feel the strength of the muscles in my horse's back and as I listen to my horse's rhythmic gait, my concentration grows stronger and stronger.

My horse and I compete as a perfect pair . . . I sit in balance and harmony as I finish my round with calm, confidence, and poise. Counting strides makes me more relaxed and I remember to breathe calmly and slowly. I finish my round feeling confident. I exit the ring feeling better than I have ever felt in my whole life. I squeeze my reins as my anchor to promote feelings of calm and confidence. I perform safely and appropriately up to my own maximum potential. I listen to my body's common sense limitations and warning signals.

This entire suggestion is represented by the letter *H* of my sub-key word, RHYTHM. Anytime I think, say, or see the word RHYTHM, all suggestions keyed to this word are automatically activated, stimulated, and work for my benefit.

Twenty minutes, wide awake.

CHAPTER 9

PEAK PERFORMANCE

Your Expectations: From Mistakes to Peak Performance

Your attitude toward defeat is crucial to mastering it.
You can see it only as a loss or as a chance for gain.

—Napoleon Hill,
Keys to Success: The 17
Principles of Personal Achievement

Do you condemn yourself for things that you did in the past? Don't worry, everyone does at some point. Perhaps there are choices you made at crucial turning points in your life that you'd like to take back. Maybe you treated someone you cared for poorly and wish you had another chance. In your riding, perhaps you made a mistake that cost you a competition and you are still angry and frustrated with yourself about it.

If you want to be successful in your riding—and in your life—it's crucial that you release the past and not blame yourself for events that have already transpired and that you cannot change.

Ask yourself this question: Has beating yourself up about the past ever helped you or made you feel better? In the ring, has it ever made you ride better? If your answer is no, this chapter is tailor-made for you!

This chapter will approach peak performance from the inside out by helping you eliminate the self-defeating behavior involved in clinging to mistakes of the past.

Choosing to Change Is Not Enough

Changing your behavior is more than just making the decision to do it. A perfect example is what most people do with New Year's resolutions. Once a year, with enthusiasm and confidence, many people proclaim: "This year, I'm going to be a more positive person" or "This is the year I'm going to treat my body better and lose those 20 pounds." They claim that acknowledging that they need to change is the first step toward achieving their goals. And that's true.

But by February 1, most New Year's resolutions are distant memories, and precious little progress has been achieved toward goals that were supposed to be of the utmost importance.

Going to Seminars and Buying Cassettes and CDs Is Not Enough

For many people, once they realize that they need some help to get over their past mistakes and achieve what they are capable of, they go to a seminar and/or order some self-help tapes. They jump up and down, clap, and cheer enthusiastically at the seminar, and then listen to the tapes every day for a week or two. Soon the excitement of their personal potential wears off and, well, they're back to where they started.

What's Missing? What's the Secret Ingredient?

Actually, there are two secret ingredients, and they work together: using the subconscious to deliver your goals, and practicing your desired physical behavior (i.e., your riding technique) and your desired mental behavior (i.e., your thought patterns). After all, what keeps many people from accomplishing their goals can usually be distilled down to one simple concept: their behavior doesn't support their goal.

What do you do if your trainer teaches you how to make better transitions? You practice it until you get it right, of course. What eludes most people is that changing the way we approach our thoughts should be handled in the same way. So if you feel like you beat yourself up over past mistakes and you want to change that thought-behavior, you'll be much more successful if you practice, practice, practice.

Fortunately, peak performance is a learned ability. It is reached on a consistent basis because of training. Not luck, not talent, and not just practice. Over time, you can move from however you are feeling and performing in a particular moment to how you need to feel at that moment.

The successful person recommends this approach. If you've done something in the past that you feel you can and should change, then by all means take action. If you've been unkind to someone, apologize. If you failed to fulfill a promise you made, take steps to fulfill that promise. If you made a mistake in competition, devote more of your practice time to whatever it was you had difficulty with.

The unsuccessful person wallows in regret and self-pity over these things and uses language that furthers the depth of his misery. Naturally, the unsuccessful person is then unable to move forward. The strategy of berating yourself for past conduct solves nothing and only serves to lower your self-esteem. You create a vicious cycle where negative experiences and negative feelings are reinforced, which leads to more negative outcomes and more negative feelings.

You aren't going to change one bit of your past. What's done is done. Learn from your past experiences and move on. You did the best you could, given your awareness and understanding of your options at the time. You are human and it is in our nature to make mistakes. You have nothing to gain from self-condemnation except feelings of misery and inadequacy.

Below are the Top 10 Mistakes Equestrians Make. I'm sure you'll find a couple—if not all—of your mistakes in the list.

Top 10 Mistakes Equestrians Make

10. Imagining failure

If you visualize missing a lead, stopping at the fence, not making a fluid transition, losing a stirrup, going off course, knocking a barrel over, or falling off at the Liverpool, guess what's going to happen?

9. Riding nervously

Your horse instantly knows when you are nervous, not because your horse has psychic powers, but because you cannot hide your feelings. Your body language, your movement, and your voice all communicate your true feelings. Your horse will pick up on your feelings immediately and become nervous, as well. So if you're worrying about something in the middle of your trail class, you'll only be negatively affecting both you and your horse.

8. Stressing about what other people think of you and your riding

"My parents are here watching me and that makes me so nervous. If I screw up, they'll stop paying for my riding lessons."

7. Making unreasonable demands

"If we don't jump this round clean, I'm selling my horse and my saddle to the first person I see and I'm taking up yoga."

6. Worrying about things you have no control over

"If a dog runs out in the middle of the ring when I'm in the jump off, I just know that my horse will spook."

5. Lacking focus

Have you ever been on course and said to yourself, "No matter what jump I'm on, I'm always thinking about that one jump that I'm afraid of and what's going to happen there." And, as you know, if you are thinking about what might occur in the future, you're definitely not focusing on the present moment.

4. Making a lot of technical errors

If you are looking down all the time or riding with your reins too long, your performance will suffer. And hypnosis won't help you if you're not aware of what you're doing. This is why it is important to work with a trainer because your trainer is able to see the patterns (good and bad) that you have developed.

Whether you are using the proper technique or not, the more you ride, the more patterns you create for your muscles. So if your technique isn't good, when you practice you are creating undesirable patterns in your brain. And the more you've practiced with your bad techniques, the longer and harder you'll find it to change them because they have probably become habits that you are unaware of.

The flip side of all of this, meanwhile, is that if your technique is good and you practice frequently, you have established motor memory (also called "muscle memory") that will serve you. Your movements are learned and stored in the brain, which then sends signals to your muscles. The result is that you will not be consciously aware of each movement or feeling, but you will somehow be doing everything right. You'll be in the zone.

Bad habits are not easy to change. The process of altering them involves being conscious about how you are moving and feeling. It requires concentration on developing new skills to replace the ones you've developed so well that they have become unconscious. And again, it requires the eye of a trainer.

If you are trying to develop a new skill, I suggest you practice it for at least 21 days. Anything less will not result in a true learning experience; your desired movement will not become automatic in a couple of days or even weeks.

3. Thinking you're not good enough to be riding at the level you're competing at

"Maybe I should have stayed in the adult jumpers for one more circuit."

2. Wallowing in negative self-talk

"I'm not strong enough to post without stirrups for more than 30 seconds; I know I'll fall off." And you will.

1. Allowing past mistakes to consume your thoughts

"I always get too close to the first barrel and I know I'm going to knock it over."

Anxiety prior to performance not only increases negative thoughts, but it also negatively affects your coordination.

Here are some exercises and tips that are useful, on the conscious level, to start reprogramming your mind from expecting more mistakes to peak performance . . .

Things to Do:

■ Focus on success. If you have a hard time stopping yourself from dwelling in the past, I suggest that you try to focus on your past successes rather than mistakes. Visualizing and thinking about past successes is an excellent way to build confidence and self-esteem. *What you think about is what you become.* Therefore, when you concentrate on your successes, you help to create future successes.

■ When you are completely relaxed and in a highly receptive state of mind, repeat the following: *I am grateful and thankful for every expe-*

rience of the past, and for everything connected with those experiences. I find it easy to let go of my fears. I forgive myself for every mistake I have ever made. Life goes on, and so do I: growing rich in experience and in the capacity to achieve. I am stronger than anything life can offer.

- Mentally rehearse. When you practice riding in your mind, you are doing more than simply visualizing. Use all of your senses, be realistic as possible, and believe in what you see.

- Model excellence. As I've discussed throughout this book, modeling is a powerful way to retrain your brain. By continually imagining the person you want to ride like, and then by putting your face on that person and making him into you in your mind, you have a real, live vision of the performance you desire.

- Embrace change. Resistance to change is a surefire way to exhaust yourself and waste your time. You must love change, desire change, and understand that life *is* change. Change is not positive or negative, it merely *is*. Your reaction to change and your relationship to change are what will determine how easy it is for you to adjust.

- Take time each day to remind yourself of how much you've improved since you first started to ride. Remind yourself of all the positive experiences you have had, of all the successes you have achieved. Tell yourself that you are brave, smart, balanced, and confident. Tell yourself that you are proud of your achievements and that you believe in your abilities. And, most important of all, remind yourself that each mistake you've made along the way has been a learning experience that has brought you to your current competitive level. When you do something well, tell yourself, out loud, "I did that well." And when you do make a mistake, make sure you look for the things you did well or correctly.

- Be deeply committed to this process. Your Positive Mental Attitude (PMA, a key Napoleon Hill concept) will keep you poised, in a state of equilibrium, and will create an environment where commitment is effortless. When you are constantly seeing and feeling the benefits of committing yourself to attaining the highest level you are capable of, those benefits and that commitment compounds. It multiplies exponentially (just as negativity and misery compound the more you indulge in them—so beware).

The Importance of Your Mind-set

Many athletes develop problems with their mind-set because they begin to overindulge in self-criticism and self-judgment. Riders, like all other athletes, can often be their own worst critics and harshest judges.

Early in my career as a hypnotherapist, I noticed a trend in the athletes that came to me for help with their performance. All of them were extremely talented, and most were already very successful in their sports; they seemed like people who should have been incredibly confident in their abilities. So why were they having trouble with their mind-set?

I began to see that it had a lot to do with the standards they were setting for themselves.

A poor or weak mind-set normally is the result of critiquing one's abilities to a fault. It's a result of negative self-judgment. When highly skilled, successful, and otherwise self-confident clients came to see me, I realized that the reason they were having so much trouble with their performance was that they were judging themselves not against other competitors or against their true selves, but against the *unrealistic expectation that they had to perform perfectly each and every time.*

The result of this pressure was counterproductive stress and anxiety that produced negative self-talk and a self-destructive attitude that took away from the quality of their performance.

Riders often believe that it is imperative to nail the "perfect spot" on the first fence, to perform flawless transitions, and to have perfect lead changes each and every time. When once in a while they don't perform perfectly, they feel frustrated, embarrassed, and humiliated. Their performance can go quickly downhill from there as they start to berate and reject themselves right there in the riding ring. All of this occurs because they expect perfection from themselves.

To overcome the problems that result from a poor mind-set, I suggest you look at yourself and your riding from a brand-new perspective. Take a step back and realize that you are in very good company. The best athletes in the world and the most successful riders make mistakes all the time. And they treat them as feedback and they learn from them.

> *Mistakes are essential to progress. The willingness to learn from them is the backbone of any progress. The object is to succeed, not to count your mistakes.*
>
> —Tae Yun Kim

Focusing on mistakes creates the fear response I discussed in Chapter 8: muscle tension, negative self-talk, inability to concentrate, and an accompanying array of other harmful reactions that stand in the way of achieving peak performance.

If you happen to chip a fence or miss a transition, remind yourself that the mistake doesn't reflect on you as a person or an athlete—it's the way you respond to that mistake that does. Let me repeat that:

Mistakes don't reflect on you as a person or an athlete—the way you respond to them does.

Joan King, a fellow sports hypnotist and NLP practitioner whose focus is on golf, had this to say in one of her seminars several years ago: "Peak-performing athletes rarely put themselves down. They talk to themselves positively about what they are attempting to create. They change past negative messages that come up into positive empowering ones. This is a part of their mental training program." She should know.

The bottom line here is that you can be the most important judge of your own performance. The most damaging criticism you can receive is criticism from yourself.

The Importance of Being Confident

The impression we have of who we are and what we might be able to achieve is developed very early in life (many experts say by the age of six). Fortunately, the self-image can be re-created; there are steps you can take to transform your negative self-image into a positive one and improve your self-confidence:

1. Acknowledge that your self-image is negative and in need of change. Like your realization that your attitude about mistakes needs adjusting, this is the crucial first step in the transformation of your confidence.
2. Make a list of things you like about yourself and your riding. Riding can be a powerful tool for improving—or damaging—your self-confidence and self-worth. Notice how rereading the items you like about your riding boosts your confidence with each read. Add items each day and reread the entire list each day.
3. Make a list of things you don't like about yourself that cannot be changed. (And then don't spend any more time trying to change them.)
4. Make a list of things you don't like that *can* be changed. (Now here's a great place to focus some energy!)
5. Create a plan for changing the items in number 4. (And in Chapter 11: Goal Setting and Achieving, I'll be discussing the process of planning in depth.) Your confidence will build as you set and achieve your goals and progress on your way to peak performance.

WARNING: There is such a thing as too much confidence. As you know, under-confidence causes negative self-talk and leads to fear of failure, self-doubt, lack of concentration. Naturally, all of this negativity prevents you from enjoying yourself and performing to the best of your ability. But overconfidence is equally dangerous as it will mislead you into thinking that you and your horse can do things that you cannot do. This can easily lead to injury, and it is irresponsible to put your horse in an impossible situation.

Designing Peak Performance

Former Brooklyn Dodgers owner Branch Rickey once said, "Luck is the residue of design." In other words, a great way to increase the likelihood of success in your riding is to come up with a plan to make it happen. Putting this plan together is a lot simpler than you would imagine, and requires only four steps:

Step 1 is to *know why you ride*. Perhaps you started out in equestrian sports because you loved horses. Perhaps you took it up for exercise. Maybe it was the competition that originally attracted you. Many equestrians after riding for a while, however, lose sight of their original intent and get caught up in the negative aspects of competition.

Riding is not only about winning and losing, it's also about being in touch with yourself and finding your unique talents and abilities. Think of riding as a metaphor for empowerment, a metaphor for concentration, a metaphor for the strength we all have but don't think we do.

As soon as you find yourself losing sight of what drew you to riding in the first place, take a moment and picture how excited you were the first time you climbed up on a horse. Remember the sights, sounds, and feelings of that day, and remind yourself how excited and lucky you still are to be involved in such a rewarding activity.

To decide your personal motives for riding, ask yourself these questions as often as you can:

- What do I want from riding?
- What do I want from myself when I ride?
- What do I want *for* myself?

Step 2 is to map out how you plan to get back into the frame of mind you established in Step 1, so that you can enjoy your trip to success. If you've ever used mapquest.com or Yahoo! maps, you know that you can ask the program to create maps or driving directions based on the shortest distance in miles, the quickest route, or the most scenic. For your "map," you want to arrive at your destination (success, improvement, winning, having fun) in the easiest and most enjoyable way.

Formulate a plan that you will enjoy executing on a daily and weekly basis. The enjoyment of riding is in the process of accomplishing, not in the end result itself. I've found throughout my life that the more I enjoy doing something, the more relaxed and confident I am, and thus the more successful I become at it.

Step 3 is having a way to define and measure your success. How will you know when you've reached your destination? Will it be when you start to win at all of your events? When you become well or better known in your discipline?

Again, try to think beyond winning and losing. In my CDs I assume that your goal in riding is to achieve peak performance, and I show you how to do this through relaxation and mental imagery exercises that target your subconscious mind. In many respects, this makes performing at your highest potential as easy and spontaneous as riding a bicycle. Just as the ability to ride a bike doesn't require conscious thought, once the keys to relaxed riding are in your subconscious, you will never again be nervous or question your riding abilities.

That being said, consider that we've all had days when we've ridden extremely well, but for some reason or another didn't place as high as we thought we should have. Conversely, there have been days when our performance fell short of our own expectations, but we nevertheless did very well with the judges. In which scenario do you experience the most enjoyment?

Keep in mind that the process of becoming a better and more successful rider is an ongoing one, and achieving peak performance simply begins with relaxing on your horse and enjoying yourself.

Step 4 is acknowledging your success. If your goal was to win a particular event and you failed, acknowledge the aspects of the event that were successful. Certainly the training and preparation you put into it was a success because you've matured and developed as a rider, ribbon or not. There might be only one first-place winner, but your efforts will lead to another, perhaps bigger win.

Because of all of the uncontrollable factors in riding, and because judging can by its very nature be subjective, you have little control over the results of an event. You do have complete control, however, over the effort you put in, and over what you find enjoyable about riding.

Let go of negative experiences and bad performances as soon as they occur. The more attention you give to them and the more emotion you attach to them, the more prominent a place they will have in your mind, and the greater the probability that they will negatively affect your future

performance. When a negative thought rises to your conscious awareness, immediately jettison that thought galaxies away, never to return.

Positive experiences and fabulous performances, however, should be
remembered in all of their splendor. What do they feel like, sound like,
smell like, look like? Attend to their every detail so you will have a strong
mental picture of what you want to replicate in the future.

Peak performance is about allowing your ability to emerge. The skills
you have manifest themselves and you are "in the zone."

The zone is a mental state of allowing everything to seamlessly come together without fear or anxiety. Being in your cylinder with nothing else
around you.

Sarah's Story

I'm one of those riders who loves to go to horse shows, but hates
the nerves that I get when I enter the show ring at competitions.
I swear I can't think when my heart is pounding in my throat. I
feel like everyone is watching me and judging me. Sometimes I'm
so nervous that the course I just spent one hour memorizing in
my mind vanishes into outer space. I end up on the course, without the faintest idea of which jump I am supposed to be heading
toward next. I just wish that I could outgrow my nervousness.

Three weeks later . . .

I've been hypnotized so that I automatically control my nerves from the subconscious level of my mind. The first thing that happens is that when I hold my reins they trigger the subconscious mind to relax and my breathing slows down to a normal rate. When I focus on my course that I am about to do, I don't feel my heart pounding hard in my throat. I also squeeze my reins together and repeat the word "relax" silently to myself. Now that my nerves are totally under control, I can remember the instructions that my trainer has given me. I am riding with much more confidence. The thing that I am most pleased about is that I no longer forget where I am when I am on course. My rounds are so much smoother and I am riding with much more control of my horse. By being more calm and relaxed, it's so easy to be more focused on my riding and remember what it is that I am supposed to be doing. Ever since I was a little girl, I always admired how Margie Goldstein rode. She was always so strong, determined, and focused. She was a rider that always knew what she wanted her horse to do, and how she was going to get her horse to complete the task. During my session with Laura, she had me visualize Margie riding and watch a movie in my mind and see all the positive aspects that I admired most. Then I did the Theater of the Mind exercise to visualize myself riding like Margie. Visualizing myself riding like Margie in my own mind is now anchored in my mind to every time I sit in the saddle. This has made me ride with more of a defined purpose. I sit taller in my saddle and feel stronger, too. My riding has improved since I have changed my way of thinking.

Self-Hypnosis for Peak Performance: Instant Alpha Conditioning

Instructions:

1. Use the word you selected to replace the alpha conditioning technique introduced in Chapter 4. Read the following script and let alpha occur.

2. Then proceed to the script for Peak Performance.

From this moment on, each and every time I desire to attain the deep state of total relaxation, I am instantly and fully relaxed, as I am now drifting into the alpha state of consciousness. The moment I think my chosen word _____, alpha occurs. This word has an effect only when I use it and only under the proper circumstances. Each and every time I do use it I am fully prepared to receive positive, beneficial, and constructive suggestions, impressing each one deeper into the storage and memory facility of my brain.

From this moment on, _____ triggers deep relaxation of my mind and body. I feel alpha occur. I feel wonderful. I feel comfortable. I am totally receptive and responsive to my own creative ideas and suggestions. I am bathed in a glow of quietness, peace, and serenity. My chosen word works only when I deliberately use it for deep relaxation to attain alpha consciousness. Its use in regular conversation has no effect on me whatsoever. From this moment on, each and every time I desire the deep state of total relaxation, I am instantly and fully relaxed upon saying _____. Because my subconscious must follow my command, each and every time I desire total relaxation, I am instantly and fully relaxed when I think my chosen word _____. I feel a deep sense of gratification as this word programming becomes a reality. Feeling wonderful, generous, alive, and eager to awaken . . .

Twenty minutes, wide awake.

Peak Performance—Building Confidence, Poise, and Self-Image

I am talented and skilled in my ability to ride well. I am a wonderful person. I take pride in what I do. I am my very best in the show ring. I am talented in my horseback riding abilities. I deserve to be the very best that I can be. I choose to perform at the peak of my abilities. I know that other people appreciate the wonderful skills and abilities that I possess.

I visualize myself riding and performing just like the person whom I admire most in riding. When I visualize my role model and admire her natural charisma and natural talent, I know that I can ride with the same comfort, ease, confidence and skill. I see myself with all of her talent. I believe that I have my role model's skills and strategies. I perform at my peak, just as my role model performs at her peak. I feel my role model's confidence and strength. I ride just like my role model rides.

Every time I ride my horse, I ride with confidence and poise. I perform with the same confidence and the same poise as my role model. I enjoy riding as much as my role model enjoys riding. I know that I ride just as well as my role model rides. I am fantastic! I am so talented and confident. I know that if she can do it, I can do it! Nothing can stop me from performing at my maximum potential.

I have the motivation and the ability to ride with great confidence and poise. I perform in just the way that I desire. I have the ability to ride well and therefore I do. I have the confidence and the skills to perform better than I ever have performed before. Each time I ride my horse I find that I become even better than the time before.

I completely enjoy what I do. I am a talented and skilled individual. When other people comment on how well I perform, I am pleased that they notice my skills. I am most pleased that I have given myself permission to be the best that I can be. I feel fulfilled and accomplished. I feel in control and relaxed. I enjoy riding and competing. I am great! I am better than I have ever dreamed possible. Each and every day, with each and every breath that I take, my riding skills get better and better.

I perform safely and appropriately up to my own maximum potential. I listen to my body's commonsense limitations and warning signals. With each breath that I take, I feel more confident and better about myself. I am a wonderful person with skills and abilities that I may not even be aware of yet. I am thankful that I discover new and wonderful things about myself each and every day.

I am important to life. I have confidence in my judgment . . . I am honest and dependable. My integrity is felt by everyone that I meet. Through my creative thinking, I direct my life to wholesome expressions. I express radiant vitality and boundless energy. I am courageous and have great faith in myself. I know that I act with complete confidence and poise. I have a wonderful self-image and can do anything I put my mind to. When I look into a mirror, it is easy for me to say something positive about myself each day. I may focus on my beautiful smile or my glistening eyes. I may acknowledge what a kind person I am. I am thankful that I can say something positive about myself each and every day. As I say positive things about myself, I become more confident.

My mind is a powerful magnet. Whatever I focus on is what I attract into my life. I focus on what I want. I see myself living the life I really want to live. I allow myself to be the best that I can be. I deserve the very best. I allow myself to experience the success that I truly deserve. I take great care of myself. I feel good about myself. I feel relaxed, comfortable, confident, and happy. I open my mind to positive thoughts. I believe that I am a winner. I find happiness in life and I enjoy myself. I am a success and I achieve all of my goals. I am always prepared for the next riding challenge. I succeed in competition and I deserve to win. My energy is boundless and I feel alive. My confidence radiates to others and I ride with wonderful poise.

This entire suggestion is represented by the letter *M* of my sub-key word, RHYTHM. Anytime I think, say, or see the word RHYTHM, all suggestions keyed to this word are automatically activated, stimulated, and work for my benefit.

Twenty minutes, wide awake.

PART III

PUTTING IT ALL TOGETHER

CHAPTER 10

DEVELOPING YOUR OWN SCRIPTS

This chapter is based on scripts of my *6 Keys to Winning for the Equestrian* series in annotated form, so you can: (1) see how I chose my words very carefully for maximum effect and; (2) be better positioned to create your own self-hypnosis CDs for whatever issues you would like to resolve or improve in your life. To review the images and anchors that I've used as examples, turn to page 43 (the Theater of the Mind), page 45 (Anchoring), and pages 55 to 64 (the Natural Laws of the Mind). Remember that when you are creating your own scripts, you'll use anchors, images, colors, and descriptive language that are appropriate for your learning style (i.e., visual, auditory, kinesthetic). If you are going to record your scripts and add music, I recommend slow music with deep tones because it will lower your pulse rate, heart rate, and blood pressure. Eventually, it will decrease your levels of stress hormones. Sounds from nature, such as rain, wind blowing through leaves, and waves can create similar effects. Sound can dramatically alter your brain chemistry, your mood, and your body, so be mindful of its effects and make your selections carefully.

R   Basic Relaxation

H   Positive Self-Talk

Y   Gaining Concentration

T   Release of Performance Anxiety

H   Fearless Showing and Jumping

M   Peak Performance

Basic Relaxation for the Equestrian

When I ride I feel so relaxed . . . I enjoy being with my horse because it makes me feel so good. I feel relaxed when I hold my horse's reins—I automatically feel so comfortable and relaxed when I am holding my horse's reins when I ride. I am able to ride well . . . I am able to be peaceful and alert while I am riding. Because I am calm and relaxed, my horse performs better. I do whatever task I need to do with such confidence, relaxation, and ease. Everything I do comes so easy to me. I find that because I am calm and relaxed on the horse I am riding, my horse responds to me better. I ride with complete balance . . . I handle everything that my horse does with great confidence and self-assurance.

I am very calm and peaceful. I feel great. I completely enjoy the wonderful feeling of being completely relaxed. Relaxation comes to me so easily, so much so that should I try to resist relaxation consciously or subconsciously, my body automatically grows more relaxed. I continue to relax even more soundly and more deeply with every breath that I exhale. I enjoy all these sensations that allow me to relax without any effort whatsoever. My whole body just gives in. The more and more I allow my body to relax, the better I feel. The better I feel, the more and more my body relaxes.

In every way now I feel better, happier, and more content. Every second, every minute, every hour, every day, my self-confidence builds more and more. I have a positive attitude. My mind stays calm and content in all situations. I have the ability to let everything flow in peace and harmony with my new way of enjoying life. I have good thinking and good judgment . . . always relaxed and able to handle all events in my life with the ability to let everything happen in a peaceful content way.

When I ride my horse I feel relaxed and enjoy being on my horse because it makes me feel so good. I ride well because I am peaceful on my horse. I am calm and my horse performs great . . . I do whatever task I need to do with such confidence and ease. Everything I do comes so easy to me. I am calm and relaxed on my horse . . . and my horse responds so well to all of my requests. I feel so comfortable on my horse as I ride with complete balance and ease. I handle everything that my horse does with such confidence.

I feel so marvelous and wonderful every time I ride . . . these wonderful feelings stay with me all the time—every day. I am happy and content when I ride. I give in to the potential of my mind and body. Whatever my mind can conceive, my body can achieve. How great I feel when I am riding . . . how peaceful. All of these suggestions help and guide me to be more and more relaxed every time I ride. I allow my body to relax and to enjoy these wonderful, good feelings that go through my body.

Anytime I desire to feel better than I do, I simply take a moment . . . take a couple of deep breaths, and say the word "relax" quietly to myself. The word "relax" is a conditioned response key to my subconscious mind. When I say this word, I recapture the feelings of being comfortable and relaxed while on my horse. I feel enthusiastic about my future.

The word "relax" is my conditioned suggestion.

Every time I use my relaxation programming, it becomes more effective.

Each time I say the word "relax" while I am on my horse, I ride with harmony, comfort, and relaxation.

Every time I have a lesson or I practice for a show I feel more and more confident. I am in balance and enjoy riding with the rhythm of my horse's gait.

I am automatically relaxed when I hold onto my reins. This makes me feel so confident, relaxed, and secure.

This entire suggestion is represented by the letter *R* of my sub-key word, RHYTHM. Anytime I think, say, or see the word RHYTHM, all suggestions keyed to this word are automatically activated, stimulated, and work for my benefit.

Twenty minutes, wide awake.

Positive Self-Talk

When negative thoughts enter my mind about horse-back riding, I mentally say the word "cancel" to myself. I replace any negative thought that I may have with a positive thought. Positive thoughts remain within the conscious portion of my mind much longer and much clearer than every before. Without fail, without exception, without excuse, each and every time a negative thought or idea enters my mind, I mentally say the word "cancel" to myself. My personal life is in order, my private life is content, and my health is in perfect order. I see myself how I want to be. I am positive, happy, healthy, and glad to be alive.

I know that being positive, happy, healthy, and being glad to be alive is called being "in the zone." I am in the zone when I ride.

I understand that being in the zone is when I feel that I am winning all of the time . . . it is an unstoppable, powerful confidence that means that I am the best that I can be. I am always absolutely doing and achieving what I set my mind to do.

I am thankful that through the power of positive thinking I have the ability to create positive actions.

My internal positive self-talk allows me to achieve whatever outcomes I want to work toward. I know that when I practice positive self-talk, my subconscious mind allows positive thoughts to flow through to the conscious mind. Every day that I ride, I am physically stronger and fitter. I am more alert, more wide-awake, and more energetic. Every day that I go to the stables, I remain so deeply interested in whatever I am doing.

When I ride, my mind is much less preoccupied with myself and I am much less conscious of myself. I focus on my task at hand. Every day that I ride, my nerves are stronger and steadier.

When I am on a horse, my mind is calm, clear, and composed.

I think clearly . . . I concentrate easily . . . my memory is sharp . . . I see things in their true perspective and do not allow them to get out of proportion.

Every day that I ride a horse, I am emotionally calm and tranquil. I feel a wonderful sense of personal well-being, personal safety, and security. I am completely relaxed and tranquil. I have confidence in myself and in my ability to ride, perform, compete—whatever I ought to be able to do. I am optimistic, happy, and confident. I stick up for myself . . . I stand on my own feet . . . I hold my own ground. Things happen exactly as I wish for them to happen in and out of the riding arena. I remain cheerful and optimistic. No matter what is going on in my life, I always remain positive and free from negative self-talk. I am confident in my riding abilities and "cancel" out any negative and harmful self-talk that I may have. I remain with a clear outlook for a wonderful and successful future in and out of the riding arena.

Every time I see the color red, it reminds me that I will be positive and in the zone.

This entire suggestion is represented by the letter *H* of my sub-key word, RHYTHM. Anytime I think, say, or see the word RHYTHM, all suggestions keyed to this word are automatically activated, stimulated, and work for my benefit.

Twenty minutes, wide awake.

Gaining Concentration for the Equestrian

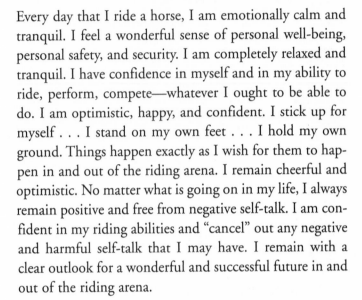

I am totally focused and attentive in my riding lessons and in the show ring. When I am riding a horse, just as a magnifying glass concentrates energy into a particular point of light, my mind excludes everything except the chosen task at hand. I am thankful for my ability to pay close attention to what my instructor is teaching . . . it is easy for me to concentrate during the classes that I compete in at horse shows. I am thankful for my ability to focus my faculties on a single purpose . . . I am thankful that I can concentrate on riding to achieve my peak performance.

I concentrate deeply and my ability to reason is alert. I know that I am a master of the art of concentration. I concentrate without effort. It is easy for me to focus and to keep my attention on my lesson or on the class that I compete in. I exclude all else from my mind, while still being certain that my well-being is foremost important.

I feel focused and attentive when I sit in my saddle. I ride with complete balance and I handle everything that my horse does with confidence and self-assurance. It is so easy for me to concentrate . . . I easily learn new skills and conquer new challenges. Concentration opens doors to new areas for me . . . I am pleased that as I gain concentration, my capacity for learning and for development expands. I am attentive to details in all areas of my riding experience. My ability to find a solution to a new challenge is rewarded with firmness of mind and clarity of purpose. I persevere until I am satisfied with the outcome of my specific endeavor.

My ability to concentrate is strengthened each time I mount my horse and sit in the saddle.

Relaxation automatically increases my ability to concentrate. Concentration intensifies my mind and increases my awareness of my surroundings. I know that I desire to learn more . . . I solve whatever problems are before me. I become more relaxed and my concentration increases as I flow with my horse's movement.

My ability to concentrate reinforces all that I learn in my lessons. I am so thankful that my ability to concentrate expands my mind.

My mind automatically executes what I successfully accomplish in my lessons. My mind is open and eager to use all of the knowledge that it gains.

I persevere with determination in my desire to concentrate thoroughly on my riding. I succeed admirably and I am pleased with my efforts. I am pleased with my ability to be attentive to details. My ability to find solutions to challenges is increased as I pay attention with firmness of mind and clarity of purpose. I persevere until I am satisfied with the outcome of my encountered endeavors. The focus of my attention is strengthened each time I use my ability to concentrate, each time I get on my horse, and each time I sit in the saddle.

The more I ride, the more I master the art of concentration. Anytime I need assistance concentrating, I take a deep breath, exhale, and say the word "focus" quietly to myself. The word "focus" is a conditioned response key to my subconscious mind. When I say this word, I recapture my ability to concentrate while on my horse.

This entire suggestion is represented by the letter *Y* of my sub-key word, RHYTHM. Anytime I think, say, or see the word RHYTHM, all suggestions keyed to this word are automatically activated, stimulated, and work for my benefit.

Twenty minutes, wide awake.

Release of Performance Anxiety

I enjoy riding in competitions . . . I enjoy performing in front of others. I am self-reliant and comfortable being a winner when I perform.

I release all performance anxiety I have ever experienced in the past . . . I release everything negative connected with those experiences. I am free from any fears of performance anxiety . . . free to be me. I accept myself completely . . . I love myself.

When I picture myself before a group of spectators, I take in a deep breath and then exhale completely. This makes me relaxed and centered inside. I smile and feel at ease as I imagine myself performing in front of others. I am confident in my ability to be calm. When, in reality, I am before a group of spectators, I take a deep breath and then exhale completely. This always makes me feel relaxed and centered on the inside. I smile at the prospect of having the opportunity to perform before others.

I am thankful for the opportunity to ride in a show to test myself against other competitors. I enjoy riding in performances in order to test my own talents and abilities. When I ride, my mind is occupied only with the task at hand. I know that I ride well . . . I know that I am skilled . . . I know that I am talented. I am well prepared to meet my goals. I give each class that I compete in my full attention. It is easy for me to focus on every corner and on every stride. I execute every move with style and precision.

I am a winner . . . I enjoy riding horses . . . I enjoy competing to test my abilities . . . My attitude is positive and full of fun . . . I focus my attention on the horse that I am riding . . . I keep my concentration as long as I want to . . . I am decisive and make correct decisions easily . . . I am consistent because I am focused . . . my body and mind are in perfect harmony . . . I give each stride my full intention and attention. I am proud of myself . . . I behave like a winner . . . I have all the traits of a winner . . . I know that I deserve to ride well

6

. . . I know that I deserve to win the class. I am a true competitor and sportsperson.

7

If a performance doesn't come off as planned, I deal with any mistakes in a calm and effective manner. I take any mistakes that may occur in stride. I do not accept negative thoughts or feelings. I handle all situations easily and effectively, which separates me from the other rid-

9

ers. I am thankful that I meet any challenge before me with ease. I am ready for any challenge. I ride with confidence and poise.

2

I am a winner. Success moves throughout my entire body and makes me feel wonderful. I give each riding performance 100 percent of my attention.

Compounding

Each successful challenge that I conquer is imprinted on my subconscious mind as a blueprint that is recalled at any moment in time.

2

My mind applies this blueprint to my mind-body connection so that my muscle me mory is always there for me to achieve peak performance.

4

I enjoy riding, performing, and competing in front of others because I enjoy sharing my skills and talents with other people. I enjoy being successful . . . I feel like a winner through and through. I am secure and confident. Positive radiance shines from me.

Compounding

Every time I want to relax before I compete, I hold my horse's reins and repeat the word "relax" silently to myself. "Relax" . . . "relax." I take a deep breath in and then exhale . . . "relax." The energy of being a winner surges throughout my entire body. I feel at ease and in total control. I am confident and calm with my competition skills. This inner warmth that I feel grants me happiness and success in the competition ring.

This special cue of holding my reins, breathing, and saying the word "relax" to myself always works for me in this way.

Whenever I need to relax and release any performance anxiety, I squeeze my reins, breathe, and say the word "relax" silently to myself. My body feels wonderful, powerful, focused, and in control.

This entire suggestion is represented by the letter *T* of my sub-key word, RHYTHM. Anytime I think, say, or see the word RHYTHM, all suggestions keyed to this word are automatically activated, stimulated, and work for my benefit.

Twenty minutes, wide awake.

Fearless Showing and Jumping

I am self-assured and confident in my ability to ride and compete. I use positive and empowering self-talk to achieve my goals. I am in control of my life. I no longer have fear-based emotions. I relax and release every fearful experience of the past and everything connected with those experiences. It is so easy to let go of my fears. My positive experiences supply me with the energy to meet all the challenges that I encounter when I ride. My subconscious mind has the amazing ability to disengage me from every negative and harmful impression ever made upon me.

I am grateful and thankful for every experience of the past. I forgive myself for every mistake I have ever made; and I forgive everyone else who may have in any way harmed me.

I know that good comes out of each experience. I forgive myself for greater opportunities and I look forward to greater achievements.

I grow stronger with each and every experience . . . I am stronger than anything life can offer. I am prepared to meet any riding challenge that I encounter in a state of mind that is free from negative thoughts.

I possess the power and the ability to channel any occurrence into a rich and rewarding experience.

I am open to new suggestions, which I accept and act upon. I am open to all the warmth, joy, and fulfillment that showing has to offer. I feel glad to be alive and enthusiastic about my future. I am thankful that I have the opportunity to show and compete. I am calm and relaxed and a sense of peace permeates my body and mind. I fully release the past fears and all the effects that these fears have had upon me. I am free . . . free of the past fear of showing . . . free to be me entirely. I accept myself completely . . . I am a valuable and talented human being . . . I am always aware of my innate worth. There are things that I do that are done better by me than by any other human being. There is no one who can exactly duplicate me . . . I accept myself . . . I love myself. I am grateful for my new level of understanding.

I easily visualize myself riding in competitions. I love the powerful feeling that riding my horse brings to me. I enjoy the harmony and balance of my horse as I hear the sound of the hooves patting the ground.

I thoroughly enjoy these feelings as I ride. I am confident and poised when I compete.

In order to prepare to compete when I am at a horse show, I go through my round quietly in my mind. My mind is serene as I take slow deep breaths and allow quiet to occupy my insides . . . I spend several minutes going over the round in my mind . . . I relax and breathe . . . relax and breathe . . . relax and breathe. Calm and trust is all that is right. If there are any unnecessary internal voices, I use counting so that my unconscious mind can assume control of my body and its reactions. One . . . relax, two . . . breathe . . . three, four, five . . . relax, six . . . breathe, seven, eight . . . relax and breathe . . . nine, ten. Counting calmly puts me into a state of relaxation. I feel composed and free of tension . . . my breathing is slow and even. When I count the strides between my fences I relax and breathe.

Showing my horse is such a pleasant experience. I become totally immersed in the experience of competing. The fluid and graceful tempo of my horse is the rhythm of my body and my horse working together.

I physically anchor the calm and wonderful feeling of competition by touching my right thumb and forefinger together as if I am holding my reins in each hand.

This is my trigger that anchors these pleasant feelings of calm and confidence as I compete. I am confident, calm, and relaxed every time I hold my reins.

3

It is calming for me to picture in my mind a successful jump or a successful go. It is easy for me to prepare my mind by simply going through my routine mentally—I visualize my round and this makes me calm. I am completely certain about the ride I am about to have.

When it is my turn to enter the ring to compete, I breathe deeply to relax my mind and body. I center my body on my horse and I become perfectly comfortable as I hold the reins in my hands, touching my anchor to calm and relax me.

I feel self-assured, light, supple, poised, composed, and confident at the prospect of a successful ride. I ride my horse with rhythm, tempo, balance, and harmony. As I feel the strength of the muscles in my horse's back and as I listen to my horse's rhythmic gait, my concentration grows stronger and stronger.

My horse and I compete as a perfect pair . . . I sit in balance and harmony as I finish my round with calm, confidence, and poise. Counting strides makes me more relaxed and I remember to breathe calmly and slowly. I finish my round feeling confident. I exit the ring feeling better than I have ever felt in my whole life. I squeeze my reins as my anchor to promote feelings of calm and confidence. I perform safely and appropriately up to my own maximum potential. I listen to my body's common sense limitations and warning signals.

This entire suggestion is represented by the letter *H* of my sub-key word, RHYTHM. Anytime I think, say, or see the word RHYTHM, all suggestions keyed to this word are automatically activated, stimulated, and work for my benefit.

Twenty minutes, wide awake.

Peak Performance—Building Confidence, Poise, and Self-Image

I am talented and skilled in my ability to ride well. I am a wonderful person. I take pride in what I do. I am my very best in the show ring. I am talented in my horseback riding abilities. I deserve to be the very best that I can be. I choose to perform at the peak of my abilities. I know that other people appreciate the wonderful skills and abilities that I possess.

I visualize myself riding and performing just like the person who I admire most in riding.

When I visualize my role model and admire his natural charisma and natural talent, I know that I can ride with the same comfort, ease, confidence, and skill. I see myself with all of his talent. I believe that I have my role model's skills and strategies.

I perform at my peak, just as my role model performs at his peak. I feel my role model's confidence and strength. I ride just like my role model rides.

Every time I ride my horse, I ride with confidence and poise. I perform with the same confidence and the same poise as my role model. I enjoy riding as much as my role model enjoys riding. I know that I ride just as well as my role model rides. I am fantastic! I am so talented and confident. I know that if he can do it, I can do it! Nothing can stop me from performing at my maximum potential.

I have the motivation and the ability to ride with great confidence and poise. I perform in just the way that I desire.

I have the ability to ride well and therefore I do. I have the confidence and the skills to perform better than I ever have performed before. Each time I ride my horse I find that I become even better than the time before. I completely enjoy what I do. I am a talented and skilled individual. When other people comment on how well I perform, I am pleased that they notice my skills.

I am most pleased that I have given myself permission to be the best that I can be. I feel fulfilled and accomplished.

I feel in control and relaxed. I enjoy riding and competing. I am great! I am better than I have ever dreamed possible. Each and every day, with each and every breath that I take, my riding skills get better and better.

I perform safely and appropriately up to my own maximum potential. I listen to my body's commonsense limitations and warning signals. With each breath that I take, I feel more confident and better about myself.

I am a wonderful person with skills and abilities that I may not even be aware of yet. I am thankful that I discover new and wonderful things about myself each and every day.

I am important to life. I have confidence in my judgment . . . I am honest and dependable. My integrity is felt by everyone that I meet. Through my creative thinking, I direct my life to wholesome expressions. I express radiant vitality and boundless energy. I am courageous and have great faith in myself. I know that I act with complete confidence and poise. I have a wonderful self-image and can do anything I put my mind to. When I look into a mirror, it is easy for me to say something positive about myself each day. I may focus

on my beautiful smile or my glistening eyes. I may acknowledge what a kind person I am. I am thankful that I can say something positive about myself each and every day. As I say positive things about myself, I become more confident.

My mind is a powerful magnet. Whatever I focus on is what I attract into my life. I focus on what I want. I see myself living the life I really want to live.

I allow myself to be the best that I can be. I deserve the very best. I allow myself to experience the success that I truly deserve. I take great care of myself. I feel good about myself. I feel relaxed, comfortable, confident, and happy.

I open my mind to positive thoughts. I believe that I am a winner. I find happiness in life and I enjoy myself. I am a success and I achieve all of my goals. I am always prepared for the next riding challenge. I succeed in competition and I deserve to win. My energy is boundless and I feel alive. My confidence radiates to others and I ride with wonderful poise.

Compounding

This entire suggestion is represented by the letter *M* of my sub-key word, RHYTHM. Anytime I think, say, or see the word RHYTHM, all suggestions keyed to this word are automatically activated, stimulated, and work for my benefit.

Twenty minutes, wide awake.

CHAPTER 11

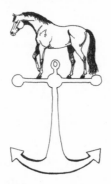

GOAL SETTING AND ACHIEVING

"Failure to Plan is a Plan for Failure"

Goal setting and achieving requires dedication, perseverance, and, most important, a plan. In this final chapter, I'll take you through the same step-by-step process I use with my clients to help them achieve peak performance in their riding. I'll begin with a question that is deceptively simple to most people: What are goals?

Goals Defined

A goal is something that you intend to achieve. Sounds simple, right? Well how about this: What's the difference between a goal and a dream? Again, a goal is something you intend to achieve. A dream, on the other hand, is something you'd like to achieve, but for which you don't have a plan. In fact, dreams can be so vaguely worded that they are not easily planned *for.*

Consider Carrie and Matthew:

> CARRIE: I want to improve my performance and achieve peak performance.

> MATTHEW: I will cut my time on my jumpers for my Grand Prix class by 10 percent and have consistently clean, clear rounds within three months.

Who do you think will achieve his or her goal? Clearly, Matthew's goal is more attainable because it is specific and allows for the creation of a time line, complete with deadlines and action steps. Carrie, on the other hand, words her "goal" so vaguely that it is more like a dream. Wanting something does not imply that you are willing to put in the time and energy necessary to achieve it. Furthermore, Carrie doesn't tell us what constitutes improvement for her or what she would have to do to "improve." Everyone wants to achieve peak performance. But people who plan for peak performance will get it, and the people who want it will probably continue to want it for a long time.

Wording Your Goals

Your goals are most useful when they are worded as outcomes. There's a lot of confusion around the word "outcome," so if you understand what it is, please bear with me. For the process of achieving peak performance for equestrians, an outcome is a specific, clear statement of what you want to be doing and thinking at the end of a specific time frame. In other words, "improve my jumping" isn't specific enough. What does "improve" look like? Matthew's goal of cutting his time by 10 percent on his jumpers in his Grand Prix class in six months is a fabulous goal because it is stated as an outcome.

Outcomes must be measurable ("by 10 percent . . . in three months") reachable (given Matthew's physical ability, his outcomes are possible), and worded in the positive ("I will . . ."). Remember the discussion of how your brain doesn't know what to do with the word "not," and how it's impossible to not picture, for instance, a purple horse sitting across from you? Similarly, creating an outcome that says "I won't fall off my horse" is a surefire way to fall off your horse.

"I will cut my time on my jumpers for my Grand Prix class by 10 percent and have consistently clean, clear rounds within three months." Now that's achievable. That's an outcome!

When creating your own goals, remember . . .

The Importance of Being Specific

State your goals as outcomes. Be as specific as possible in describing exactly what it is you will be achieving. Your outcome should be measurable, reachable, and worded in the positive.

The Importance of a Time Frame

Putting a time frame to your outcomes is what allows you to develop a plan. You may want to travel across the country, but if your time frame is to do so in one day, that information is going to significantly affect your plan for travel. Goal-setting programs typically categorize your outcomes as short-, mid-, or long-term goals. Short-term is usually one year or less, mid-term is usually one to five or ten years, and long-term is anything thereafter. Fortunately you don't have to wait that long to see results with this program.

I use the following time frames: one month, three months, six months, and one year. So I define short-term goals as *outcomes that will be achieved within one month*. And I use a worksheet that looks something like this:

ONE MONTH

1. Your Physical State
2. Positive Self-Talk
3. Your Focus
4. Your Emotional State
5. Your Mental State
6. Your Expectations

THREE MONTHS

1. Your Physical State
2. Positive Self-Talk
3. Your Focus
4. Your Emotional State
5. Your Mental State
6. Your Expectations

SIX MONTHS

1. Your Physical State
2. Positive Self-Talk
3. Your Focus
4. Your Emotional State
5. Your Mental State
6. Your Expectations

ONE YEAR

1. Your Physical State
2. Positive Self-Talk
3. Your Focus
4. Your Emotional State
5. Your Mental State
6. Your Expectations

Your Goals Will Come Out of Your Challenges

Once you have clearly written the challenges you have in each of the six areas I have addressed in the book (i.e., your mental state, your emotional state, your fears, etc.), you will be able to formulate outcomes. The premise here is that of the road map—you must know where your starting point is in order to most effectively reach your destination. Your directions for travel are your plan.

Based on the above, brief introduction to outcomes, list three outcomes you are going to use this program to achieve. You might revise them later as you gain clarity about the process, so don't be attached to them.

Outcome 1:_____

Outcome 2:_____

Outcome 3:_____

At Summit Dynamics, I use the ACHIEVE system for outcome creation, planning, and achievement (what most people refer to as goal setting). It's simple, it's very easy to remember, and you can do it all by yourself in the privacy and comfort of your own home.

The system below takes advantage of hypnosis's ability to turn suggestions into behavior, and NLP's program for manifesting the outcomes you desire. This is where we integrate hypnosis, NLP, and your own unique abilities and wishes, and produce what you have defined for yourself as peak performance.

The ACHIEVE System

A = Action
C = Create
H = Human
I = Identify
E = Energy
V = Visualize
E = Evaluate

A = Action

Before outcomes, before plans, comes something very simple: deciding that there are things about your riding that you need to change. This is a pivotal moment because that decision is not meaningful until you commit yourself to take action.

C = Create

To get the outcomes you want, you need to make a plan, right? Well this is where you create your starting point. This is where you define exactly where it is you are right now so that you can develop the most effective, efficient plan to where you'd like to go. To create the optimal affirmations and outcomes for yourself, use the following as a guide to creating your starting point. I'll use the example of my client, whom I'll call Debra, to help you understand how this process works.

WHY DO I NEED THIS PROGRAM?

> DEBRA: I'm performing so poorly because I still can't get over that my husband wants a divorce. I constantly think about it and I'm sure it's partially responsible for how badly I'm doing. And my previous trainer and I had a pretty bad falling-out and I get so tense whenever she's around that I practically freeze up. I haven't improved at anything and I don't even enjoy riding anymore.

Now you try . . . .

Why do I need this program?

_____

_____

_____

_____

_____

1. Your Physical State from Tension to Relaxation

> DEBRA: Every time I know I'm going to a show I get nervous. I just know I'm going to see my old trainer. Boy did we end on bad terms, and I feel she's going to be laughing at me for trying to show. I was so attached to her as my trainer and when she quit teaching me over something that I had nothing to with, I was devastated. It was so hard for me to even think of riding with someone else. I know that when I get to the show she'll be watching.

NOW:

_____

_____

_____

_____

2. Positive Self-Talk

DEBRA: I can't ride well enough to show. . . I'll really screw up when I see my old trainer. . . . When I go into the ring and start cantering I'm just going to mess up, I know it. . . . I never remember the trail class; it's so hard to get around. . . . I can't afford this with everything else going on in my life.

NOW:

_____

_____

_____

_____

3. Your Focus

DEBRA: I'm scattered every time I see all the other horses practicing and going in both directions. . . . I have a hard time keeping my mind on what I'm doing. . . . I keep thinking about what I need to do to get my divorce.

NOW:

_____

_____

_____

_____

4. Your Emotional State

> DEBRA: I get so anxious when I have to perform. I love rid-
> ing and I want to show but I get so worried and just can't
> imagine that I can really do it. . . . I'm so frustrated all the
> time and I cry all the time. I guess I have to admit that I
> still love my husband in a way; I've been married for 15
> years. I think maybe I worry too much about negative
> things happening.

NOW:

_____

_____

_____

_____

5. Your Mental State

> DEBRA: I just left my husband. After years of verbal abuse,
> it was time to like myself and leave. Now I'm worried if I
> can afford to pay for my horse. But since my horse is my
> lifeline, I have to figure it out.

NOW:

_____

_____

_____

_____

6. Your Expectations

> DEBRA: I'm so fat, I'm sure I look terrible on the horse. . . .
> I'm just not good enough to be doing this. Everyone at the
> show is better than I am.

NOW:

_____

_____

_____

_____

H = Human

Recognizing your humanity is an integral part of this program. We make mistakes, we have a tendency to be critical and hard on ourselves, we have difficulty forgiving the faults of others as well as ourselves, and have a really hard time releasing bad memories.

Without getting too much into psychoanalysis, much of how we act and react was formulated during childhood. How did your mother or father respond to adversity? Were they competitive? Were they hard on themselves or on you? When did they compete, with whom, and why? How did they respond to others? Were they immediately trusting or not? What did winning mean to them? How did they feel about the person who cut ahead of them in line?

Now how about you? How do you respond to adversity? Are you competitive? Are you hard on your parents or on yourself? With whom do you compete and why? How do you respond to others? Are you immediately trusting or not? What does winning mean to you? How do you feel about the person who cuts ahead of you in line? If you don't place as high as you wanted, whose fault is it? The judges, the horse, the golf cart that went by, or was it just meant to happen the way it did? Is there a pattern between your parents and yourself?

If there is, the first part of acknowledging your humanity is to Release and Clear whatever feelings you have about your parents and their influence on who you are today. Let's face it: You can't do anything about the past anyway, so allowing it to adversely affect your thoughts and your performance isn't all that effective as a life strategy.

In addition, reread your responses in the C = Create section and note if you are blaming anyone for anything or if you are concentrating on mistakes, bad relationships, or negative feelings from the past. For instance, here was Debra's response:

DEBRA: I need to forgive my soon-to-be ex-husband, my former trainer, and myself.

What about you?

_____

_____

_____

We all have choices to make every day of our lives. Choosing to be happy and keeping yourself relaxed and calm is one of those decisions. Forgiveness is, too. Let me repeat that: forgiveness is a conscious decision. Happiness is a conscious decision. Take responsibility for your own state of mind. After all, you're the only one who controls it.

I = Identify

Now that you've laid the groundwork toward moving past the past, it's time to create the future. It's time to identify the affirmations you'll be using throughout whatever time period you choose for your outcomes. Through self-hypnosis, you'll go into alpha and repeat your affirmations, which compound the effects of your suggestions (affirmations) so that they're even more powerful than when used on the conscious level. You'll find you are able to reach your goals even faster when you combine your effectively written affirmations with the power of auto-suggestion.

We'll use Debra's challenges as examples of how you can transform your negative thoughts into a system for changing your behavior and achieving your outcomes.

YOUR PHYSICAL STATE: FROM TENSION TO RELAXATION

DEBRA: Every time I mount my horse at a show I am calm, I breathe freely and easily, and I am completely relaxed. Each time I see my former trainer I feel great about myself.

POSITIVE SELF-TALK: FROM NEGATIVE TO EMPOWERING

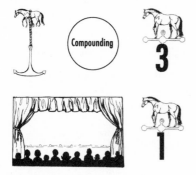

DEBRA: Every time I sit in my saddle I realize my natural talent and I ride well. I easily recall all of the details from all my practice sessions and my performance is flawless. I visualize myself doing the entire trail class exactly as it's supposed to be. I enjoy myself and my horse responds positively to everything I do.

YOUR FOCUS: FROM SCATTERED TO OPTIMAL CONCENTRATION

DEBRA: Each time I see another horse in the practice area or in the show ring, my focus increases. I easily stay in the present and all of my concentration is on the task at hand.

(Note: Debra's initial response was to create an affirmation that would help her refrain from thinking about her divorce. Upon attempting to word that affirmation, however, she realized that it was impossible to create one that alluded to NOT thinking about her divorce without actually thinking about her divorce every time. Remember—stick with positive thoughts.)

YOUR EMOTIONAL STATE: FROM ANXIETY TO THE ZONE

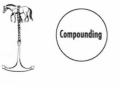

DEBRA: I am positive and relaxed every time I perform and I easily and quickly reach the zone. I choose to be happy and look at life in a positive light.

YOUR MENTAL STATE: FROM FEARFUL TO FEARLESS

DEBRA: I am recognized as being great at my job and I am always well compensated for it. Money comes easily to me and I'm fantastic at managing and growing my money. I am grateful for the abundance in my life.

YOUR EXPECTATIONS: FROM MISTAKES TO PEAK PERFORMANCE

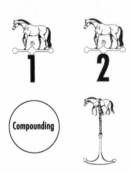

DEBRA: I am slim, trim, and I look fabulous on my horse. Every time I hold my reins, I am confident and self-assured that I can do anything I put my mind to.

E = Energy

To cultivate optimal physical abilities you need to have your body in the best physical condition to ride. This means paying attention to your energy levels and what affects them.

- Do you get adequate rest?
- Do you eat well?
- Are you getting plenty of exercise?
- Do you avoid negative people?

You need to be aware of how your body responds to your environment and react appropriately to any signals it sends you. When you learn to have complete body awareness, you are able to ride with more rhythm and fluidity. Remember Natural Law 7: Reactions Must Be Managed. How you react to what is around you affects your health and your performance.

V = Visualize

It's time to make your own home movie out of your outcomes; this is when Theater of the Mind is most helpful. See everything about your outcome, from every angle, including panning around the environment and zooming in on yourself as well as your horse. Zoom in on all of the spectators as they are in awe of your performance, and in awe of how fabulous you look on your horse. Feel the excitement of making every jump, clearing every barrel, or remembering every detail of your trail course.

E = Evaluate

Evaluation is a critical component to success and should be scheduled into your plan to achieve peak performance. Points of evaluation in your plan allow you to decide if the manner and direction in which you are progressing is acceptable to you. And if it isn't, it gives you the opportunity to regroup and redirect: to chart a different course or use a different strategy and continue in the same direction.

The rationale for building points of evaluation is that those points prevent you from going too far in the wrong direction. If you wait too long to evaluate your plan and your progress, often there is so much wrong with what you are doing that you can't pinpoint the initial place or time when you veered off plan.

This is what I suggest: evaluate your plan and your progress once a week. Decide in advance what progress looks like so you know if you have reached it. It doesn't have to involve anything more sophisticated than a "yes" or a "no."

For example, when Debra was asked to write about one of her goals and how she would evaluate it, she wrote:

> *In three months, my focus and concentration will improve to the point where I am positively affected by the presence of my former trainer, and I think of my financial and personal future positively. I know that abundance and peak performance are my destiny. I will set the stage for my outcomes by doing Release and Clear every day, followed by Gaining Concentration, for 21 days. I will practice what my trainer tells me to work on for at least 45*

minutes per day, knowing that once I have done what he tells me to do 21 times I will have created a new, more positive habit. I will go to a small schooling show in three months, enjoy it immensely, and I will place in my class.

Debra has created many points for evaluation. Each week, she either did her Release and Clear and Gaining Concentration or she didn't. And she either practiced for 45 minutes or she didn't. Either she made the necessary arrangements for the schooling show or she didn't. These are simple points that demonstrate her commitment to doing the work she needs to do to reach her goals. And if she hasn't done them, she'll know why her goals haven't been reached. As Pat Riley says, "There's no such things as coulda, shoulda, or woulda. If you shoulda and coulda, you woulda done it."

Success is Rarely an Accident

Frank Lloyd Wright once said: "I know the price of success: dedication, hard work, and an unremitting devotion to the things you want to see happen." If you have that unremitting devotion and you are dedicated to putting in the work you need to follow the steps of your plan, success will be yours because you believe it already is . . .

A Final Word

Acknowledging that you need to change something (or maybe closer to everything!) about the way you ride and the way you think about your riding is the vital first step toward achieving peak performance. Take pride that you've taken that first step and take pride again for each step you take hereafter. I think of that trite saying that I used to find very annoying: you get what you pay for. It's true, though. Your outcome is usually in direct proportion to the amount you were willing to "pay" for it: in energy, in time, in work, and in thought.

There is no magic elixir for peak performance. But there is a process that combines the technology of the mind with the teaching of a great trainer. As long as the subject (that's you) is willing to do his or her part, the odds of achieving peak performance increase exponentially. Here are my final recommendations:

■ Create a Daily Riding Journal to not only help you keep track of all of your progress, but to also keep track of your thoughts and feelings about taking responsibility for reaching your goals. In addition to monitoring whether you practiced, did your self-hypnosis sessions, and maintained a good attitude, you can respond to the following:

1. The best part of my riding today was:

2. My feelings during my lesson or while shoeing today were:

3. What I learned about my riding ability today was:

4. I learned the following about myself today:

5. I learned the following about my trainer today:

6. I learned the following about my horse today:

7. I am grateful for these things in my life today:

■ Please note that in my experience, the only time optimal results are clearly not forthcoming in this process is when my client doesn't communicate well with his or her trainer. Clarify what you are being asked to do—several times if necessary—so you completely understand the whats, whys, and hows of your trainer's expectations. If you don't, you'll be sabotaging your own process, and although you'll probably be quick to blame your trainer, you will be the one who is ultimately at fault.

■ I cannot emphasize enough that you should set standards and goals that are very specific, and that points of progress keep you in check (if you have created them effectively). And that, above all, you should value your progress so much that you are brimming with pride for your achievements.

The buck stops with you. You owe it to yourself to avail yourself of all of your resources: your trainer, your horse, and your entire mind and body. I wish you the best of luck and I hope you will give yourself the gift of peak performance.

Smiling makes you feel good; it stimulates
chemicals in your brain that elevate your mood.

Smile more often!

INDEX

A

ACHIEVE System, 195–204
affirmations, 132–33
alpha conditioning
  concentration, 120–22
  fear, 148–51
  performance, 167–70
  performance anxiety, 135–38
  relaxation, 80–84
alpha state, 11, 24
analytical mind, 13
anchoring, 45, 131–32
anger, 35
animal magnetism, 7
attitude
  choice and, 61
  effects of, 27–28
  of gratitude, 64
  reactions and, 62
auditory processing, 46–47
authority figures, 26
autosuggestion, 76, 97–98

B

Bandler, Richard, 31–32
behavior modification, 38
belief systems, 17
beta state, 10–11
body functions, 14–15
Braid, James, 7, 76

brain, 9–10
  alpha state, 11
  beta state, 10–11
  delta state, 12
  mind and, 12–27
  theta state, 11–12
breathing, 71–72, 131, 145

C

cause and effect, 49–50
change, 54–55
Circle of Excellence, 42–43
color, 73–74
communication, 35–38
compounding, 85
concentration, 109–10
  ACHIEVE System, 201
  alpha conditioning, 120–22
  definition, 110
  distractions, 112–14
  examples, 115–20
  exercises, 114–15
  learning, 110–11
  loss of, 111–12
  scripts, 178–80
confidence, 162
conscious mind
  critical factor, 23–24
  functions of, 12–15
  mental-conditioning laws, 39

properties of, 22, 24
subconscious and, 19–21
critical factor, 23–24

D
danger, 19
daydreams, 18–19
delta state, 12
disgust, 36
dreams, 18–19
Dyer, Wayne, 52, 56, 64

E
Elman, Dave, 9, 23
emotions, 17
    communication and, 35–38
    management of, 62
    physical reactions and, 57–58
energy, 202
Erickson, Milton H., 8–9, 32
eternal present, 53–54

F
fantasies, 18–19
fear, xiv, 27, 36, 139–40
    ACHIEVE System, 202
    alpha conditioning, 148–51
    burnout and, 142
    conquering, 143–44
    definition, 140
    examples, 146–48
    exercises, 144–45
    irrational, 140–41
    physical manifestation of, 141–42
    scripts, 183–86
feedback, 38
free thought, 51
frequency of impression, 60
frequently asked questions
    hypnosis, 5–6
    Neuro-Linguistic Programming, 33

future, 59–60

G
goals
    ACHIEVE System, 195–204
    challenges and, 194–95
    definition, 191–92
    specificity, 193, 205
    success, 204
    time frames, 193–94
    wording of, 192–93
gratitude, 64
Grinder, John, 31–32

H
habits, 17–18, 59–60
healing, 8
Hill, Napoleon, 60
human relations, 52
humanity, 199–200
hypnosis, xi–xii, 3–4, 29
    attitude and, 27–28
    critical factor and, 23–24
    fears and phobias, 27
    frequently asked questions, 5–6
    history, 6–8
    modern, 8–9
    self-control and, 24
    waking, 25–26

I
ideas, 63
images, 58
imagination, 19, 58
impressions, 59–60
information processing, 48
    auditory, 46–47
    kinesthetic, 47
    visual, 46
injuries, 147–48
intensity of impression, 60

K
kinesthetic processing, 47
King, Joan, 161

L
language, 8–9, 89–107
laws of the universe
    cause and effect, 49–50
    change, 54–55
    eternal present, 53–54
    free thought, 51
    human relations, 52
    perception, 53
    work, 51–52
life experience, 20–21
love, 37

M
meditation, 5–6
memory
    conscious mind, 14
    exercise, 21–22
    subconscious and, 18, 20–21
mental-conditioning laws, 39
Mesmer, Franz Anton, 6–7
mesmerism, 7
mind
    conscious, 12–15
    laws of, 55–64
    subconscious, 15–19
mistakes, 126–27, 132, 161
modeling, 41–42, 130, 159
muscle tension, 73–74

N
negative thinking, 60–61, 128–29
Neuro-Linguistic Programming, 31–33
    frequently asked questions, 33
    practice, 34
    principles of, 34–40
    techniques, 40–48

O
outcome, 38

P
patience, 127
perception, 39–40
    attitude and, 61
    law of, 53
perfection, 92
performance, 153–56
    ACHIEVE System, 202
    alpha conditioning, 167–70
    confidence, 162–63
    designing, 163–66
    examples, 166–67
    exercises, 158–60
    mind-set and, 160–62
    recommendations, 204–6
    scripts, 187–89
    Top 10 Mistakes, 156–58
performance anxiety, xiii-xiv, 123–33
    ACHIEVE System, 201
    alpha conditioning, 135–38
    examples, 134–35
    exercises, 128–33
    scripts, 180–83
Perls, Fritz, 32
phobias, 27
physical reactions, 57–58, 141–42
plasticity, 60
positive thinking, 55–56, 60,
    128–29, 159
practice, 60, 79
present, 53–54

R
rational function, 13–14
reactions, 62
reasoning, 13–14, 17
relaxation, 67–68, 200
    alpha state and, 80–84

basic, 85–87
compounding, 85
examples, 74–76
exercises, 70–74
scripts, 174–76
self-hypnosis, 76–80

S
Satir, Virginia, 32
scripts, 173–74
concentration, 178–80
fear, 183–86
performance, 187–89
performance anxiety, 180–83
relaxation, 174–76
self-talk, 176–78
self-hypnosis, 9
alpha state and, 80–84
basic relaxation and, 85–87
compounding, 85
rules for, 77–79
self-talk and, 102–7
self-knowledge, 45–47
self-talk, 89–90
ACHIEVE System, 201
alpha state and, 102–3
changing, 92–93
definition, 90–92
examples, 98–102
improvement of, 97–98
positive, xiii, 93–94, 106–7
release and clear, 103–5
scripts, 176–78

words to avoid, 94–96
words to use, 96
state of mind, 25–26
subconscious mind, xiii, 8, 15–19
conscious and, 19–21
memory exercise, 21–22
properties of, 22, 25

T
television, 26
tension, 68–70, 200
Theater of the Mind, 43–45
theta state, 11–12, 24
thoughts, 63
trauma, 16–17

U
unconscious incompetence, 39–40
user's guide, xiv–xv

V
visual processing, 46
visualization, 129–30, 203

W
waking hypnosis, 25–26
willpower, 14
work, 51–52
working memory, 14

Z
zone, the, 123–24